VOICE OF MANY CRYING

by
John S. Munday

**Forewords from
Central America and North America**

**Skipjack Press, Inc.
Ocean City, Maryland**

COVER ART: KATHY MUMFORD, Ocean City, MD

Library of Congress Cataloging in Publication Data:

Munday, John S., 1940-
  Voice of Many Crying
    1. Theology
    2. Conversion - Christianity
    3. Central America - Christianity

ISBN 1-879535-03-3 Paper

Published by   SKIPJACK PRESS, INC.
               OCEAN CITY, MARYLAND 21842

Printed in the United States of America

To Fran, who understands
accompaniment and conversion, and
who lives that understanding with me.

WHY AM I HERE ?
Why am I here in El Salvador,
to see the pain, to cry once more?
Tell me please why it is true
that these dear people must be so blue?
Why am I here to see the pain
that falls on them like storms of rain?
Why am I here in this distant land?
Could it all be part of God's plan?
Why am I here? It's plain to see
that my sisters and brothers want me to be.
Why am I here? I have no choice,
as they cry out to me to be their voice.

Fran Munday
El Salvador, 1987

ACKNOWLEDGMENTS

I would like to give special thanks to the following people who have been so important in my life and who gave of themselves to make this book possible.

My wife, Frances Wohlenhaus-Munday
When I came back from my first trip to Central America, I said Fran could go to Nicaragua, but El Salvador was too dangerous. She went to El Salvador within 4 months and has been leading me ever since. To Fran I owe deep gratitude for many helpful suggestions and hours of reading. She made this a better book.

Mark Kline Taylor
Mark gave me much direction and encouragement during the writing of the first draft of this book as my Thesis for a Master of Theology Degree at Princeton Theological Seminary. Mark went to Central America with me.

Geffrey B. Kelley
Geff began encouraging me at Princeton Theological Seminary where he was a visiting professor. He continued to accompany me as he gave his time to several revised drafts in spite of the workload he carries at LaSalle University.

INTRODUCTION

There is a saying about Central America that I first heard from Mark Taylor, that everyone plans to write a book after their first trip, an article after their second trip, and actually tries to do something to help the people after the third trip to Central America. After half a dozen years with more than one trip each year, I have come back to those feelings on my first trip and to the compulsion to tell others about what I have seen.

There are two Forewords in this book because I have come to understand that it is helpful to view each region from the perspective of the other. Jon and Hugh do that so well in these Forewords, and they each identify the source of the hope that is found among the voiceless. Also, there is an Afterword because I met Phil Mitchell just two weeks before his untimely death and I found in him and in his life the precise spirit of conversion that I am seeking to describe.

I have written this book for two reasons. First is that I have been converted. I am no longer an observer of life, both here in the United States and also in Central America. I am a participant. I am compelled to tell the story of my experiences, generalized and merged with other similar experiences. It is reassuring that these feelings we have when we first return from true conversion in the third world are normal and good and to be encouraged. We are changed, and it is important to acknowledge that change so that others will understand us better and so that others who also are changed will recognize a fellow traveller.

The second reason for writing this book is more important. Those of us who have heard the voices of the poor cry out cannot deny that voice and remain honest in our faith. I believe that God is with the poor, suffering and crying out in a loud voice. I believe that those of us who are not poor and are not threatened by violence and death daily must either speak out in a voice which is clearly on the side of those with whom God is found, or we are denying God.

This book is structured on these two reasons. Chapters One and Two look at conversion, and at the transition from observer, on a first trip, to participant, even to confrontation with deadly fear. Chapters Three through Six look at salient points which generalize the experiences of many who have experienced this conversion. In these chapters, four salient points will be examined. These experiences have been selected and set out as formative for the experience of the task forces, delegations, and exchange visitors who tell their stories back home in the United States.

Let me state emphatically that we have encountered radical evil in Central America, which was open and blatant in a way that is seldom encountered by those of us of privilege in the United States. In the face of this radical, systemic evil, there is a unique combination of suffering and joy. People survive in ways we are not accustomed to seeing, and people are joyful in that survival.

As one sees suffering and joy in the presence of radical evil, dialogue takes place with the larger church and with the government. Both in Central America and back home in the United States, governments exert powerful influences on the people. As the larger church seeks to minister to these same people, conflict arises, both between organizations and within individuals. People who seek first the kingdom of God, whether here or in a third world, are asked to make choices.

One of these choices is to say yes to the campesino family who asks us to be their voice and tell their story. As Christians, not only are we to follow Jesus, we are to tell His story. We are to tell the Gospel. We are to be a voice, a voice of many crying. That is what this book tries to do.

Jack Munday
Ocean City, Maryland

CONTENTS

FOREWORD FROM CENTRAL AMERICA

I have read *Voice Of Many Crying* with great pleasure. The reason is that it is not just another report on a trip to Central America. Neither is it an account of a series of visits, more or less separated in time, to these peoples who, despite their geographical littleness, are today on the front pages of the most important newspapers in the world. The reason for my pleasure is that I have found this report to be, throughout, a description of a personal experience of conversion, arising from contact with peoples and groups who seek to live their lives in such a way as to make the Reign of God a reality.

You can go to El Salvador, or Nicaragua, or Guatemala, with a bit of morbid curiosity, to see poor, oppressed peoples who are unjustly dealt with on a national and international level, and the trip can be a good lesson. It can be instructive. It can clear up certain unknowns, or grey areas, in the reports we read about these peoples. On the other hand, if we visit or live in El Salvador, the Central American country I know best, with an open heart, a heart free of prejudices, and not feel we have the solutions to their problems in hand -- if we simply wish to accompany the people of this land in their death and resurrection -- the result will be like the experiences of which we read in these pages. It will be an experience that transcends the physical experiences we encounter, to be transformed into an experience of life, of hope, of God.

And the poor will be transformed into the Servant of Yahweh. Like that prophetical personage, the poor have sought to bring forth justice and righteousness to the nations (cf. Isa. 42:1,56:1), and like him their fate is death (Isa. 53:12). Today the poor meet their end "with an appearance so marred, beyond human semblance" (cf. Isa. 52:14), that they are persons "from whom others hide their faces" (Isa. 53:3), because they are ostracized, impoverished, and annihilated by the sins of the mighty (cf. Isa. 53:10). So very often -- we need only recall the massacres in El Salvador and Guatemala --"like a lamb that is led to the slaughter, and like a sheep that before its shearers is silent," the victims here are prevented from so much as opening their mouths (Isa. 53:7): they have been deprived even of a voice with which to make their complaints heard. They are accounted as malefactors, and buried as transgressors (cf. Isa. 53:12), subversives, godless men and women, stripped in death of their very dignity. Isaiah's great prophecy becomes sheer reality. The poor, the oppressed, are, today, the crucified: whole crucified peoples.

Amidst such horror, God says: "I have observed the misery of my people...and I have come down to deliver them" (cf. Exod. 3:7-8). In Egypt, many centuries ago, God intervened. God intervenes today, as well, in our lands, and will continue to do so in the future. God is still the champion of the poor and oppressed. Thus, it is in the power of God that our peoples rise up and demand their rightful place on earth. The God of the Bible is the God of the poor and the oppressed. As long as we are part of God's struggle in behalf of the poor and oppressed, as long as we remain part of God's project for peace, justice and integrity, God will always be with us, and our experience will be a transcendent one: the experience of God.

One who journeys to El Salvador with an open heart,

and without prejudices -- as will be demonstrated in the pages you are about to read -- perceives the God of the poor present in the hope that fills the hearts of these "least ones." And to find hope in today's world -- especially among the poor, oppressed people, whose faces and bodies reflect the injustice and poverty they suffer -- is to have an experience of God: a God present in the midst of a people organizing for struggle and survival, a people who want to survive in order to be able to contribute to the building of the Reign of God, which is a Reign of justice, peace and freedom. We discern the "mustard seed" of the Reign in the beginnings of a new community of love, of hope, of sharing, of self-assertion. We find this community wherever the people rise up in solidarity to defend the rights that God has bestowed upon them, and to unmask and counter the evils of imperialism in all its forms and practices.

The hope that animates our communities, as the pages of this book will recount, is hope in a restoration of the fullness of life that we do not now have. We assert, along with our communities, that Jesus has "come that they may have life, and have it abundantly" (John 10:10). Therefore anything that diminishes life, or prevents it, or makes it difficult to live it to the full, is not from God. It is an evil, and we must condemn it. On the other hand, we must support, and proclaim as a sign of the presence of Jesus and the coming of the Reign, all that nurtures life.

As Peter says in his First letter, we must give an accounting of the hope we have within us (1Pet. 3:15). The Gospel is more than a denunciation of sin. It is also a proclamation of what we believe and hope. It is a message of hope amidst violence and war. And it is a summons to conversion. We have been called to choose between the idols of death and the God of life. All of us Christians are confronted by the same challenge: to reject the idols of corruption and death. May we choose the projects of God's liberation, which is revealed in the sufferings, the struggles, and the hope of the poor.

As Christian men and women, persons of faith -- and even simply as human beings--we must listen not to the voice of the politicians, who present us with the idols of death, but to the voice of our conscience, which ought to reflect the call and the interests of the God of life. We have different experiences of conversion. For some of us, crushed by oppression, conversion occurs when we feel compassion for these sisters and brothers of ours who share our suffering. In our joint struggle for life, we feel the inner presence of Christ, and we hear his promise of salvation.

For others among us, conversion begins with the painful discovery that we have been part of the cruel, merciless forces that oppress others. Once again, it has been the suffering of our sisters and brothers that has enabled us to make the discovery that Saul made: that we have been persecuting Jesus.

Whatever be our starting point, we have been invited to enter by the narrow gate:

> *For the gate is wide and the road is easy that leads to destruction, and there are many who take it. For the gate is narrow and the road is hard that leads to life, and there are few who find it. (Matt. 7:13-14)*

From out of the midst of crucified peoples--from El Salvador crucified and agonizing, but with signs of resurrection--we demand to know: Why do they persecute us? Why do they murder an innocent people, condemning the poor to death by starvation and slaughtering the defenseless? Let them cease to oppress us! And let them cease to justify inequalities in the name of Christianity, or in the name of their own freedom and security! Let them not murder our hope. Let them cease to provoke our desperation. This will not assure their salvation! Let them beware of the wrath of God, lest it be executed through the people of God. We invite them to beat their swords into plowshares, to convert their wealth into bread for everyone, their propaganda and lying into education, their total war against us into peace for all.

I find in the pages of *Voice Of Many Crying* something we hear from these crucified peoples themselves: Do not be smug in your conviction that you believe in the true God. Do you believe, really believe, in the God of Jesus Christ, the God of the poor and the "least" (cf. Matt. 25:40,45)? This God is not neutral. God is not on both sides. The Bible reveals to us a God who takes sides with the poor and the slaughtered. No Church that means to be faithful to God can avoid taking sides.

Finally, we in El Salvador have something to say to Christians caught up in this struggle, as well as to the prophetic Church: Be strong. Be determined. Remain faithful to the whole Gospel, and to God's constant, continued calls to conversion and renewal. We are summoned to follow Christ on the way of the Cross. Amidst suffering and death, we declare that we are co-creators of a new world and a new human community. Let us continue to resist the temptation of the false gods and idols, and let us make the cause of the poor--of the "least," which is the cause of God--our own.

Jon de Cortina, S.J.
Chaletenango,
El Salvador

FOREWORD FROM NORTH AMERICA

Paradox confronts us when we turn to the recent history of Central America. We see continuing outbursts of life amidst terror and violent death; we see the lives of many North Americans becoming linked with those of poor Central Americans, even as their government continues to arm those who oppress and repress the poor. And, with these linkages, the lives of North Americans are often transformed. Jack Munday's moving personal testament in this book is just one instance of such a transformation.

The outbursts of life occur among the poor -- in the Christian Base Communities, in the popular organizations (struggling for land, homes, education, unions, human rights, woman's rights, native people's rights, etc.), in the communities and towns of repatriated refugees, and among the refugees who have come to the United States. This has happened as many of the poor have come to recognize that the dominant social and economic structures of their countries are unjust, and that, through community building, they can contribute to transforming not only their personal lives but also the social structures.

In the words of Gustavo Gutierrez, the poor have "irrupted" into history, claiming their place as agents in the shaping of their own history. Their movements and projects express such values as cooperation, participation, sharing, compassion -- the values of the Kingdom of God, in contrast to the individualist, competitive and discriminatory values that are reflected in the predominant institutions. These movements, affirmed Segundo Montes, one of the murdered Jesuits of the University of Central America in El Salvador, are the seeds and the promise of genuine democracy in Central America. They represent possibilities for social transformation that cannot be recognized among the privileged, who regard only themselves as sources of historical innovation. Among the people in these movements the power to love is manifest, and the power to convert those who engage with them. No wonder they have to be killed. What their lives represented challenges to the core the moral character of the privileged elites, and threatens to displace the structures that sustain them.

How are we to explain these outbursts of life? The poor themselves cite the presence of God among them, the God who promises "abundant life," who takes sides with the poor, the oppressed and the marginalized, and who sets people free -- the God of life who confronts the idols of death. Facing repression and death, some of the poor in Central America have chosen exile, some to enter the armed struggle, and some to continue the process of popular organizing within their countries. In the process, martyrs have been numerous, and prophets have arisen to interpret the paradoxes stated at the outset.

Many North Americans have been touched, whether through involvement with refugees, through participation in solidarity groups, or through spending some time actually present among those suffering the violence. Doing so, they too have made contact with the God who is present among the poor. And they are set free, able now to live lives as participants with the poor, rather than merely to observe them. It is indeed ironic that poor Central Americans, who fifteen years ago were remote from U.S. consciousness, have been the agents who have brought renewed life to this country. But, looked at from the Biblical perspective of the Central American poor, it makes obvious sense.

For he grew up before him like a young plant, and like a root out of dry ground; he had no form or comliness that we should look at him, and no beauty that we should desire him.

He was despised and rejected by men; a man of sorrows, and acquainted with grief; and as one from whom men hide their faces he was despised, and we esteemed him not.

Surely he has borne our griefs and carried our sorrows; yet we esteemed him stricken, smitten by God, and afflicted. (Isaiah 53:2-4)

Jack Munday's life was transformed from being an observer into being a participant. In this book he brings the voice that he has heard in Central America, the voice of many crying -- but also, the voice of many announcing a better life -- to a wider audience. He speaks in the most compelling way, giving his readers insight into his own transformation. His words are worth listening to.

Hugh Lacey
Professor of Philosophy,
Swarthmore College.

1

FROM OBSERVER TO PARTICIPANT

The campus of the University of Central America in San Salvador, El Salvador, was busy with activity on November 16, 1990. Many people had arrived for the events which commemorated the murder of the six Jesuit priests and the two pious women, just one year ago that day.

Preparations were being made for an outdoor mass, at one end of a parking lot. Prayers were said as international visitors on the campus made visits to the tombs of the priests in the Romero Chapel. Tears were shed as visitors walked through the small exhibit of the personal effects of the murder victims, seeing broken eye glasses, a pipe, books and blood soaked soil.

The memory of Genesis 4:10 screamed out,
And the Lord said, "What have you done? The voice of your brother's blood is crying to me from the ground."

Some of the visitors and students walked behind the

buildings to the roped-off garden and wall where the final
killings were carried out. A rose garden had been planted.
Music was playing over a loudspeaker by Grupo
Teosinte, providing a background of song and music as visitors
mixed with students and with Salvadorans from the city and
from the campo. Small groups gathered to discuss, to reflect,
to remember, or to just sit.

I was lying back on the grass under the shade of a tree,
listening to the music and the voices of those who walked by.
I could see the bright blue sky and the high clouds, and
remembered being a young boy who knew clouds and sky but
none of the horror of murdered priests. I was young so long ago.

But, as they say, that was then and this is now. I was in
El Salvador, no longer isolated in the suburbs of North
America. I was with a group of nine from Philadelphia,
which we had named the "homeless delegation." We were in
El Salvador to exchange thoughts and, as one of our group had
early observed, had come to cross borders together in
solidarity.

In a sense, we were an unusual group for El Salvador
because we included homeless advocates and nuclear and
armament protestors who had not been involved with Central
American issues. We were black and Hispanic and white,
very young and sort of old. In another sense, we were like all
North American delegations, visiting but separated from the
murder and death that was part of this small country. We
had organized early in the year and had come together as a
group during our time in El Salvador.

The night before we had marched with thousands of
people in a memorial procession from the park next to the
Cathedral which housed Monsignor Oscar Romero's tomb, in
center city San Salvador, to the Jesuit tombs here at the
University. Most of the delegation had stayed on campus all
night, taking part in the easy family of mourners, taking part
in the mass said at the hour of death. Only two of the nine in
our group were Roman Catholic, but all of us and all of the

mourners worshipped and prayed to the same God. Such is the theology of accompaniment.

Earlier that morning before I found my spot on the grass, I had a brief conversation with Padre Jon de Cortina, S.J., as we both walked in the park. Father Cortina had visited with our group in Philadelphia some months before. He was on sabbatical from the University, and was working in El Salvador, in Chalatenango, between trips, as he had been when his six co-workers and the two women were murdered. He had just accompanied several hundred from "Chalate" for the commemorative events. Padre Cortina was pleased to know that the group had been able to make the trip. He wished us well.

As I lay under the tree, listening to the music, watching the clouds, my reverie was broken by the Simon and Garfunkle song of the 1960's, *The Boxer*, coming over the speakers, sung by Grupo Teosinte in Spanish. The music sounded so right as I lay there, echoing years off my life. The words were for today, however, for the Salvadorans of the 1990's.

I thought about how being here at the University of Central America was so different from where I lived in the United States. The song was changed, from one boxer's struggle for dignity to a people's struggle for dignity.

I remembered the words Padre Cortina spoke to our group in Philadelphia. He had said, "If God is not with the people of El Salvador, then God is nowhere." I would quote those words the next day during a day long meeting of activists and internationals.

The words were true and, as Padre Cortina would be the first to admit, God is very present in El Salvador. The good news is that we who visit El Salvador can meet God, and not only hear the Gospel but see and taste and smell it being lived by the people with whom God lives. It is a transforming experience. In this world of much confusion and rapidly changing events, there is comfort in knowing that

God is with us.

The First Trip

I made my first trip to Central America in November, 1986 as part of the Presbyterian Church (USA) Task Force commissioned by the 1986 General Assembly of that denomination. I traveled with a small group to El Salvador for five days and then to Nicaragua for five more days. Others went as small groups to Guatemala and Honduras, and then we all joined as a larger group in Nicaragua. Our report has now been received by the 1987 General Assembly. It is a permanent part of the work of the Church as it seeks to understand the presence of God in our world today. I was the rookie on the task force, and had the least background in Central American issues of anyone selected.

The Task Force was selected in accordance with all of the denominational requirements in mind. I was chosen partly because I have been an attorney for more than twenty years, partly because of my theological training, partly because of people I called on to help, and, to a greater extent than any, because of Providence. I was not selected until the last moment, and then only because a white male elder became ill and was unable to make the trip. I was the only one left on the reject list who fit the slot. I had a lot to learn.

There is a learning curve in any experience, where a great deal of basic information is assimilated and where certain issues and questions are formed and answered almost at the same time. For example, one learns that there are Sandinista and then wonders who they are, only to quickly learn, in 1986 at least, that they were Nicaraguans who came to power in 1979 as a result of a revolution that had been going on for a long time. The length of time given by an individual for that revolution to have succeeded, I have since learned, depends on the amount of sympathy for the revolution and the degree of credit given to the Sandinistas for its success in overthrowing the Somoza dictatorship.

As I took my first baby steps on the learning curve for Central America, as I joined the denominational task force delegation in November, 1986, I took part in a series of briefings just before we were to depart for the region. We met many experts of many persuasions, all of whom knew more than I did about Central America. They did not all know more than I did about logic and the truth.

The most dramatic person to speak to us was a United States State Department representative from the Office of Planning who, it can only be described this way, sauntered into the briefing room. He had a scuffed leather flight jacket, dark glasses, Eddie Bauer fatigue pants and a gold watch. As he was introduced and his think-tank affiliation was explained, he sat down in the chair and unfolded into a casual position of indifference. He was not quite as cool as Bogart, and not as alert as Harrison Ford playing Indiana Jones, but he had to have both in mind as he created his image.

The "State Department Official" (as we were instructed to identify him if we quoted him) made a vital contribution to the briefing as he characterized Central America as a region of the world where violence is unusually severe. His response to the question of why it persists was telling. He said it was internally generated and externally supported. It was not until later when I was higher on the learning curve did I realize that United States policy makers have known all along that external support is necessary for the violence to continue.

During that dialogue with all of our many experts, my Central America learning curve merged with my experience in my law practice. My thought at the time was that we were not being given any credit for independent and critical thinking. Our briefings were in some cases pro forma as it was just a matter of going through the motions, abeit in some cases with a cool and laid-back style.

As one who came into the debate over Central America in the middle of that debate, I had to work hard to understand the past. I have done that work. I believe I have been able to contribute sufficiently to the specific work of the church to justify my having been selected. I know that I have been transformed by the experience.

I have also been humbled by the opportunity to share in the suffering and joy of the people of Central America, as they struggle against radical, systemic evil. I have been called to speak out and to tell others what I have seen. I have been unable to avoid telling all who would listen, both in the larger church and in the government, about the presence of God in that little corner of the world. I experienced that presence in a way that is often not possible in the United States.

The more experienced members of that denominational task force were helpful to me as I made my first trip. They became friends on this first of many trips. It was a good beginning, and provided a good foundational methodology for my education into Central American affairs. I was told that our purpose was not to preach but to listen. We never argued with anyone who spoke to us, even if what they said contradicted what we knew or thought we knew.

The last planning session before we left focused on the group's integrity, on the goals of the task force, and on the credibility we would have with the people at home. The first page of my first notebook records my thought that "I don't know what this means yet but it is clear that everyone is trying very hard." We did try hard. Delegations travelling now to Central America try hard. I prayed, "Lord, we have been fully briefed. Each has made a sacrifice to go and each one is filled with expectations. Lord, protect us, open our eyes, and let us see through your eyes."

We went to Central America in order to hear and to look and smell and taste and touch what we found. As poverty and war and oppression torment whole nations, we were making a small attempt to *be there*, to be with the people. As I look back, I see that others who have had more experience in Central America helped me in that process. But they too had been transformed.

To Be A Voice

We were going to Central America, not to bring the truth, but so that we could walk and talk with those who were struggling with democracy and revolution and the other issues of our generation, not only in Central America but in North America too. It was a truly transforming experience. I went as an observer and I came back as a participant.

A banner made by advocates of the "sanctuary" movement symbolically depicts God breaking through barbed wire as God enters into history in our time. It was certainly in my mind as I went to Central America that I would at least figuratively be looking for Christ in the people of El Salvador and Nicaragua.

The figure of Christ was in my mind during the time we spent in a small settlement in El Salvador, outside the town of Suchitoto. The community is named El Barrio, and it was formed by the effort and determination of a group of displaced people to return to their land of origin at any cost.

In August, 1986, less than three months before our visit, refugees had returned to their land of origin in a dramatic display of courage, without permission from the Government and in defiance of the military warning that they were entering a conflict zone. Internationals who accompanied the returning community were expelled from the country by the Salvadoran Government.

Already, in the short time, the campesinos had built houses and latrines, and crops were planted. In 1991, it has been virtually impossible for a delegation to visit El Barrio. Internationals have to go one or two at a time, at times when the Army is not paying attention at the checkpoints. There is constant conflict in this region between the Army and the guerillas who have been fighting the civil war.

On that first visit, we were told that the only freedom in El Salvador is to choose the prison in which one would live. When we arrived in El Barrio we found it isolated, remote from the city, and with the road controlled by the Army. We were told that it was in a conflict zone, a nice modern word that sanitizes the murder that takes place in war and in the name of national defense. It was necessary to have a written pass which was examined at five different check points.

The day of our visit was a day of celebration because this was the one day of the week that the priest was allowed to come to minister to the people. We were invited to stay for mass and to participate in the people's worship of the Lord. We were excited to hear this and the people of El Barrio were excited to have us be a part of this celebration of their faith in the God of life in the midst of their suffering and death.

During the mass a choir member spoke of our visit as being like the visit of the wise men who went to Bethlehem, to Christ in the manger in the poor stable. When I had the opportunity, I acknowledged that we weren't bringing gifts and weren't really wise. I said that we came not to bring gifts but to meet them and to learn from them about their life so that we could tell the people in the United States what we saw.

Of course, the people were right as I look back on the events of that trip and the many since. If the place where one finds God is El Salvador, then those who travel to see that incarnational presence are making a journey not unlike the journey of the Magi. I reacted as a polite North American, seeing them describe us as the visiting wise men bearing gifts, and I knew we didn't bring gifts with us on this trip. I didn't see the Biblical analogy clearly as it is seen by the Salvadorans who live the Bible. I didn't yet acknowledge the truly incarnational power at work in their struggle to bear the pain of injustice that filled their lives.

One man's eyes lit up as he heard my words of protest translated. He smiled and reached to touch my hand. He said, "You are our voice! We cannot leave here. We cannot tell the world what is happening to us. Tell them. Tell the people in your country about the war. You are our voice!"

The sincerity of that man's plea and the strength of his grip on my hand was transforming in and of itself, even as the entire trip was transforming. Two men, each unable to speak directly in the other's language were able to so very powerfully communicate the full depth of human emotion. "You are our voice!" This was and remains still today a life changing re-enactment of the Gospel.

A Religious Experience

The process of transformation is not an easy process, and it's not something that takes place without the presence of the Holy Spirit. I had been commissioned in my home church, just before leaving for Central America on my first task force trip. Almost two weeks later, riding in the back of our tour bus in the mountains of Nicaragua with seven others, I sat, alone in the back, lost in thought. I was quite depressed.

We were coming down from the Matagalpa region and returning to Managua. We had seen poverty and war and horror on the two week trip. What good was the trip? What good could I do? I thought of home, and of my family and friends. It was 5:15 p.m. at home, and I thought about the denominational meeting being held in my home church at that time. I wondered if anyone would mention the task force.

As I thought about the bus and about home, and as I reached the depths of pain, the words of the 23rd Psalm came to me. I was comforted.

I had a Bible with me, and I read the 23rd Psalm, though I know it by heart. As I read it, I truly was comforted and I did feel that my soul was being restored. I, and the bus, were on paths of righteousness. I struggled with whether or not to involve the others in my thoughts. I remember at the time telling myself that the comfort of the word of God must be shared. It cannot be kept inside.

Finally, at 6:30 p.m., as we came near to our hotel, I asked that the bus stop. We were one block from the hotel. I told my friends about my thoughts, and how I had been depressed by all that we had seen, but that the 23rd Psalm had been comfort, and that I wanted to and needed to share this comfort with them. We stood in the bus and recited the 23rd Psalm together as a group and as a prayer.

For us at that moment it was a genuine religious experience. But it was more than that. Two days later, I called my wife, Fran, to let her know how the trip was progressing and to give her a message to be read on Sunday at our church. I asked her if anything had been said at the denominational meeting.

Fran said that for a while nothing was said, and so she asked someone if an announcement would be made. That was at 5:15 p.m., just as the words of the 23rd Psalm came into my mind. Then Fran added that the prayer for us was not until after supper, at 6:30 p.m.

At that moment, as the moderator of the Presbytery meeting in my home church was speaking to the Presbytery about the task force and asking for prayer, God was very much with all of us. The Lord's Spirit was with us, in Presbytery and in Central America, in a way that is not often appreciated, even when we talk of solidarity with the poor.

From Observer To Participant

Fourteen months later, in January, 1988, I traveled that same road from Matagalpa to Managua again, and I was in the back of another bus. This time, I was not in despair. The poverty and war was the same, and the promise of peace was more remote. And yet, I was with the people, and I saw the spiritual table which was before them, in the presence of their enemies.

I was reminded of Psalm 23 and my religious experience and I was reminded also of the feeling of despair I had the last time on that road. I realized that I was not the same person and that my experiences in Central America and at home in the United States had moved me from observer to participant. I had been transformed. And while I have had and would have many more moving experiences, I had become an active and committed participant. No longer was I an observer.

As a footnote, I should add that we received a FAX from a group in Nicaragua on September 23, 1991, telling us that we couldn't travel to Matagalpa. The letter stated, in part:

"We cannot receive you in the clinics in Matagalpa by now. More or less, since a month ago, there has been a boom of assaults and violence in the north region and we are not sure you will be safe in Matagalpa. There are a lot of new armed groups both former contras and members of the Sandinista Army. They are starting again to promote violence, killings, assaults, robberies, kidnappings, etc.

We are most sad for this situation because we are losing that peace which took so long to achieve. Besides, there is a gang which robs all vehicles that go through the North Highway since two weeks ago."

This is the same region I visited in 1986 and 1988, and the road is that road where I was comforted. Now it is closed. Once again I need to reflect on Psalm 23, and be comforted in the presence of my enemies, those who cause "violence, killings, assaults, robberies, kidnappings, etc."

2

GENERALIZING THE EXPERIENCE

As I have reflected on my experiences, and have talked to others who have been to Central America, I have generalized that no "Christian" can come back from Central America without being transformed and without telling the essentials of the same story in some way. By this generalization, I mean that people of faith who visit the region are moved by the presence of God in the circumstances of the people of Central America, and that God's presence there is real and alive and transforming. At some point in every case, there will be a moment when that person will recognize the living gospel in Central America.

In the presence of radical, systemic evil, facing death and poverty and corruption, there is something that arises, in the suffering and in the joy of a people, that is religious. It is an experience that is difficult to ignore, and when the events are mixed with Bible study and prayer, it is impossible for people of faith to remain untouched.

The reports prepared by delegations and task forces

cannot be appreciated without understanding that all of the group members have been transformed from observer to participant. Each one has had, I am convinced, the presence of God's Holy Spirit actively working in his or her life as each one has traveled and reflected and interpreted, so that each person has been transformed. This is essential to know. The words that are spoken by these truly changed persons can be understood properly only by understanding that God has been at work in their lives in a way that is not found very often in the United States. It takes much understanding on the part of those to whom the words are spoken. This may help explain why the report received by the Presbyterian Church (USA) calls for every member of the entire denomination to fast and pray for peace in Central America.

A young man who traveled with me on a delegation that Fran and I led in 1988 said that he too had been transformed from mere observer to participant. He was asked what that meant to him and he said he had been praying intensely, but had not yet fasted. Yet he understood how fasting would be a natural result of the experience.

Knowing that active participants in the experience of the people of Central America are not observers is important in order to understand their perspective. They are not neutral and are not unbiased. How could one be unbiased in the presence of God?

Of What Are We Afraid?

People in the U. S. have a reluctance to fast for peace in Central America. Some do not believe the testimony of those who have gone to the region. While the Commissioners to the Presbyterian Church (USA) General Assembly voted almost unanimously to adopt the report and its findings, many people have difficulty facing and accepting what is being said.

Fairly soon after I had returned from my first trip to

Central America, I heard a lecture by the Reverend James Goff. He had just recently retired after 37 years in Latin American missionary work. His last several years were in Nicaragua. During the discussion, Goff asked: "Why don't people believe us when we come back and tell what we have seen? We are just ordinary Christians who have nothing to gain by not telling the truth. We are telling the truth. Why don't people believe us?"

At the time, I did not have an answer to his question; but not long after that, I had an experience which helped me to answer Goff's question. It came as so many answers come, not from books but from our own reality.

At 2 A.M. on Christmas morning, our daughter's house caught fire. Lynn and her husband and two children escaped without serious harm, but were unable to save any of their personal possessions. They moved in with us for a few days until the insurance company provided temporary housing. They were helped initially by their church and our church and other groups, and have since been able to rebuild and replace much of what they lost.

Almost three weeks after the fire, Fran asked me why I had not gone out to the house to see the damage. They were beginning to rebuild and repair the damage. I had welcomed the children and grand-children into my home and had helped as I could, but I had not driven the 17 miles to their burned out house.

Why? Because I was afraid. I was not afraid for myself, obviously, but, in 1973, my step-daughter Julie (from my first marriage) died at the age of 16 from complications arising from hepatitis. In 1979, Fran's daughter Marlys was murdered at the age of 18. I just could not look at another loss. I was afraid to see how close Lynn came to death.

Yet in Central America, death and tragedy are a significant part of life just as they are for us. People are often afraid to see death in the stories that good Christians bring back from Central America. People are sometimes fearful, too, of seeing their presuppositions, prejudices, and previous beliefs die because the untruth of these beliefs is recognized. How else does one explain the reluctance of good people to acknowledge the evil of a government policy that brings death and not life?

Emancipation

This issue of fear became more clear to me when, on another visit to Nicaragua, I visited with the Reverend Gary Campbell, who is Jim Goff's replacement in Managua. During our dialogue, Campbell asked another question. With the same sense of frustration that Goff expressed, Campbell asked, " What are people afraid of? "

Once again I returned to the story of Lynn's Christmas Day fire. I have already said that I was afraid of death for Lynn and her family, but that is only part of the answer. I needed to go deeper into the analogy, to look for the relational ties. I needed to answer what was the more basic question, to know what people are afraid of.

In my notes from a different trip to Nicaragua, I have comments by Miguel D'Escoto, the Maryknoll priest who was the Foreign Minister of Nicaragua during the Sandinista administration. At a meeting in Managua, he said "...that ordinary people become accustomed to a modality of relationship, such as that which has existed between the United States and Central America. In time that modality became vital. As mighty as the United States is, it has become very frightened and a victim of fear. Fundamental control is needed and to have this, one must convince others that there is no alternative." He added that "Nicaragua was showing an alternative."

As I thought about what D'Escoto had said, it occurred to me that he was talking about emancipation. For one thing, our daughter Lynn was emancipated. She was happily married, with a husband and two children, and since the fire she has given us a third grandchild. We parents gave up control over her life, willingly yet reluctantly.

Is this not what the people of Central America are asking the United States to do, to let go of control over them? We do have great control in the case of El Salvador, for example, where we give more aid than the national budget of that country. We had parental control in Nicaragua in 1856, when the United States citizen William Walker became president of that country. We had parental control when we supported Somoza's tyrannical reign in 1933. It lasted until the Sandinista revolution of 1979. We had control when we conditioned massive aid on the outcome of the 1989 elections, which brought change to the government of Nicaragua.

A parent ultimately lets go, if not totally, at least enough so that the son or daughter can have a good, healthy, and independent life. We Christian parents trust God enough to let go. But did I trust God enough to let go of Lynn's security? Do the people of the United States trust God enough to let go of Nicaragua, or Guatemala, or the security of the region? Is self-determination too great a risk even for the most powerful nation on earth?

Central America is like much of the world. It wants to be adult and independent. Nicaragua's Foreign Minister Miguel D'Escoto said that he wanted to come in the front door of the United States and use the familiar "tu" instead of the formal "usted." He wanted to come in, not stand at the front door with sombrero in hand.

He wanted emancipation, and the right to make his own life, like Lynn and her family do. This may be our biggest fear. Didn't Lynn almost die due to an electrical fire that no one expected and was I really free to let her live in that house, at least in the darkest corner of my soul? Wasn't that why so much United States money went into the election which removed D'Escoto's party from power? And aren't *they* who hear what the poor of Central America want really afraid that the house might burn down right in our back yard?

A Deadly Response To Fear

Those who don't believe what we report when we return from our visits to that region may be refusing to believe out of fear. The fear is not so much of death as fear that the nation or region will, in its emancipation, turn out to be different than what we want. I was unreasonable in not going out to see Lynn's burned home. But it was a harmless sin, and a harmless fear. I do believe in emancipation and I have helped them unconditionally.

There is another kind of response to this fear, however, not just by the persons who have to listen to the stories of returning travellers. There is a response by those in power, those who have the parental fear that emancipation is too much to give. Sometimes that response to fear is unreasonable. Sometimes the response is truly horrible. Sometimes the response is deadly.

Our "homeless delegation" had an opportunity to visit with a group in the city of San Salvador. They had organized in a community and had struggled for dignity and opportunity. The earliest part of the community was almost as old as the war, dating back to 1981. As more people had been displaced, both from the countryside and from the city, room had been made for others.

As we visited with the community members, we were invited in to a set of buildings. As is common in Central America, the meeting room was outside, under a roof but without walls other than the side of the building to which it was attached. There was a long crude bench serving as a table in the center of the room, and benches and chairs all around. This community had been occupied during the 1989 offensive. The bombs and machine guns rained death on the women and children as well as on the men, even though they were not part of the fighting. They talked about the memory of war, and the fear that no place was safe.

A woman holding a child told us that several of her family had been killed. A man talked about his memories and about his fear that another offensive was about to start. We were startled with that thought, that we might be present during a major offensive. We weren't supposed to be part of the war.

Then the woman spoke to us again. "You know," she said, "that the killing of the Jesuits and their co-workers was not only an attack on the Jesuits. It is also a killing of the church."

The man spoke up. "The murders of the Jesuits was planned by the Salvadoran military, with the complicity of the U.S. Embassy."

"What do you mean?" we asked. As I sat there listening to this indictment, I could feel the twisting of my stomach. This was not what we wanted to hear.

"It is known. The murder of the Jesuits was planned by the military with the complicity and approval of the United States Embassy." He asked, "How is it possible that your taxes are killing, not only priests but thousands in the war?"

We had no answer, but only a sick feeling that this just is not right. I know that I felt fear and I didn't want to be told that my country had any part in the horror and tragedy of El Salvador. I didn't have a response, and no one in our delegation offered one.

What we did have was another story to take home, to tell to those who don't believe and who are afraid to believe what we say. We have a story indicating some official United States Government involvement in radical evil. I should add that this story was told to us several times and by several groups. It is a story of a response to fear, and a response to emancipation by those who will go to unreasonable means to retain control. We have a story in which those who seek emancipation and an alternative way of life were killed to prevent that alternative from succeeding.

We don't know first hand if the U.S. Embassy or even one person connected with it had anything to do with the murder of the Jesuits. We don't know if the stories are true that have been printed in the United States newspapers about certain persons at the United States Embassy having information and withholding some or most of that information. Even in July, 1991, newspapers such as the Philadelphia Inquirer were carrying stories about what United States Major Eric Buckland knew and said just before, during and just after the killing of the priests and women at the University.

The bulk of Major Buckland's January 12, 1990 questioning has been kept secret. We don't know what is being withheld from the Salvadoran court which investigated the murders, withheld in the name of National Security. We may never completely know these stories. What we do know is that there is a violent struggle taking place in El Salvador and in other places in the world, where death is being used to prevent emancipation or self determination. What we do know when we reflect on our experiences is that truth is not being told, and that death does seem to be a response to fear. Is the United States very frightened and a victim of fear? Is fundamental control so important to those in power that death is needed to convince others that there is no alternative?

Salient Points

With all the fear and disbelief of what is said, the fact remains that people like me come back with stories to tell. To understand what we are saying, it is necessary to reflect on the experiences which they represent. The experiences of those who are transformed from observer to participant are focused in certain salient points in this reflection. I have tried to bring the totality of my experience and that of others into readable shape for discussion and further understanding.

The list of our experiences is not complete. No one could tell all of the stories and relate all of the events that go into a visit to two or three Central American countries. The selection of salient features of our visits is designed here to help organize the experience. Also, it allows the selection process to be evaluated with a set of criteria against which experiences of others can be judged.

Those experiences which others might have and which have been excluded can also be evaluated later in the light of these pertinent events. These experiences have been selected and set out as formative for the experiences of task forces, delegations, and exchange visitors who tell their stories back home in the United States. In the next four chapters, these points will be examined. At the outset, however, let me state emphatically that we have encountered radical evil in Central America, which was open and blatant in a way that is seldom encountered in the United States. In the face of this radical, systemic evil, there is a unique combination of suffering and joy. People survive in ways we are not accustomed to seeing, and people are joyful in that survival.

As one sees suffering and joy in the presence of radical evil, dialogue takes place with the larger church and with the government. Both in Central America and back home in the United States, governments exert powerful influences on the people. As the larger church seeks to minister to these same people, conflict arises, both between organizations and within individuals. People who seek first the kingdom of God, whether here or in a third world setting, are asked to make choices. Dialogue with the larger church and with the government are major parts of the experience which is described here .

It is hoped that what follows will give the reader a closer view of the experiences and even allow a sharing of these experiences. The transition from observer to participant is described as an encounter with suffering and joy in the presence of radical systemic evil, shaped in dialogue with the larger church and the various governments.

As a first step in describing this transition, let us consider what is meant by the presence of evil that grated so harshly on our sensitivities on the various trips to Central America.

3

THE PRESENCE OF RADICAL EVIL

The first salient feature of what the people we came to love must confront is radical systemic evil. While evil is present in all nations and in all peoples, nevertheless it is clear that radical evil is present and acting in Central America in ways and to a degree that those who visit find it to be a dominant shadow over all their experiences. Radical evil can be overwhelming in all of the countries of Central America.

Early in the "homeless delegation" trip, we visited with some families who had been displaced by the conflict and war during the 1989 offensive. As we met with them, each of us shared our own personal stories. We were making connections as we crossed borders together. One of the women mentioned that her son was killed by the soldiers and left lying in the street. She just briefly mentioned him, as though she could not let his memory go.

When it came to her turn during the introductions, Fran told about her daughter having been murdered. A little girl

came over and said, "I'm sorry your daughter was killed."
She sat with Fran.

Soon it was Hilda's turn to introduce herself. Hilda
said that she was from a city with a lot of violence, and that
her oldest son had been murdered in a homeless shelter, five
years ago on that day. She started to cry, as did others of us.

The little girl started to stroke Fran's hair, and put her
hand on Hilda's arm in sympathy. The woman then added
that when she went to claim the body of her son, she was
stopped by a newspaper reporter for one of the daily papers
in San Salvador. He asked her to comment on the war. She
said that she responded by asking him if he would print
what she said.

"What would that be ?" he asked.

"I would say that my son was murdered by the military
for no reason," she replied. "He wasn't armed, he wasn't part
of the rebels, he was non-violent. Will you print that?"

"I can't," the reporter answered.

The woman told us that she had said, "Then get out of
my way and leave me to bury my son."

These conversations happen all the time when one
visits with the poor and those who have been marginalized.
Mothers whose sons fight in the war, either for the army or
for the guerrillas, can expect that their sons might die.
Mothers who are really poor and in the way of the conflict
can expect death even without reason. Hilda later said that
she knew the pain of the death of a son, but she could not
imagine having to claim his body from the street.

The Evil Is Systemic

We do not need to generalize from just one example of
one conversation with one group. This moment was personal to
us and was very compelling. Yet, every group in every country
meets persons who have stories that are just as personal and
compelling for them. It is systemic.

In Honduras, for example, nearly all of the women in many on the villages closest to the Nicaraguan border have had at least one child by the time the woman is 19 or 20 years old, and that child is fathered by a soldier. A man with a gun can and does take whomever he wants. It is not a question of morality for the women, but of necessity. It is not a question of romance, but of force. In the 1980's, three armies occupied the countryside, and the father could have been a Honduran soldier, a Contra from Nicaragua, or a United States National Guardsman. Many of the soldiers have left, because of the Nicaraguan peace and the Gulf war, but their children remain. For the most part, only the mothers care.

In San Juan de Limay, Nicaragua, one of my friends asked why all four of his group have been housed with families in which a member of that family had been killed by the Contras. He was told by Methodist mission co-worker Philip Mitchell that every family in the entire village had lost at least one member of their family to the Contras. In other regions of Nicaragua, every family in an entire village might have at least one family member fighting with those same Contras, but even in these places, there has been death in every family.

In Guatemala, in the Chimaltenango region in January, 1988, a baby was crying in an orphanage, one day after losing parents to what is politely called "the violence". This cry of a new orphan happened within days of a meeting of the five Central American Presidents in San Jose, Costa Rica. The Government of Guatemala claimed at that meeting that there was no conflict and no death and no war, claiming it has met all the terms of the Arias Peace Plan which was signed amid the violence.

In El Salvador, perhaps the most fragile country at this time, the government and the army has used "low intensity conflict" to cause death to civilians, using the euphemistic language of another conflict, Viet Nam, to "drain the sea" by bombing the countryside. Even now as the peace talks continue in 1991, refugees and people of the resettlement projects are bombed and international relief supplies of food are halted, to spoil or delay before reaching the poor in the countryside.

Arguing With Reality

As part of the process of travelling in Central America and in seeking to understand what is happening and why, there are opportunities to meet with many persons who are willing to express their point of view on events in the region. The President of El Salvador, Jose Napoleon Duarte, gave us an interview in November 1986, in the National Palace. As this was only a month after a major earthquake, the palace showed cracks along the walls and stairs, and repair work was going on. We were led to a large room with comfortable chairs set in a large oval.

President Duarte was very gracious and spent more than an hour with us. Duarte had been a part of the conflict in El Salvador, from the 1960's and sought to place himself in the center of the political spectrum. He claimed that the left had tried to kill him and that the right claimed he was a Communist. During the conversation, Duarte said that he had inherited the social leadership of El Salvador, but that there was also a military leadership and an economic leadership which was not under his control. To the contrary, he stated that he hoped to lead the military by example. He related how he had just visited the National University where a demonstration protested his policies. He was proud that he had responded without violence and hoped that the Army would learn from this.

Similarly, his influence over the economic sector was limited by the budget of the government. He said that the relief that was being sent as a result of the earthquake allowed him to give the government employees a raise in pay. Near the end of the meeting, Duarte made an observation that seemed to capture the reality of this tiny country. He said that in his country "there are 50,000 people who live better than most people in the United States, and 5,000,000 people who are extremely poor in the country."

President Duarte's observation summarized the polarization of the nation. The rich go to Miami to shop on a weekend. The poor can't even buy corn for tortillas. Radical evil is present everywhere, as people starve or die from lack of medicine or sanitation. It is this vivid presence of radical evil that begins the transformation process, from observer to participant.

Also in November 1986, I met Padre Jon Sobrino, S.J., at the University of Central America in San Salvador, El Salvador. Professor Sobrino acknowledged that his perspective was that of a theologian. He suggested that in countries such as El Salvador, theology uses reality, not theory, as an argument, dealing with life as it is observed and experienced, in order to find meaning in history. Sobrino contrasted that kind of theology, namely the interpretation in physical terms of what God is speaking to us in specific events, with the more formal, classical theology in which the reflection is more intellectual.

That conversation with Professor Sobrino was important to me as I have been working through my own theology and the methodology for its use. In the face of the radical evil we encountered, we who travel to Central America are exposed to so much "reality" that it becomes necessary to engage in intensive theological reflection on the events of our trips. Much of this book was originally a Master's Thesis as part of my Master of Theology program at Princeton Theological Seminary. My thinking has been directly influenced by that conversation with Professor Sobrino, and by other conversations with him, as well as reading much of what he has published in English.

My experience with reality has formed the basis of the methodology used here. In this book, I am making an attempt to balance a very compelling and transforming exposure to raw reality with an analysis of what others have thought about this reality. Starting with an encounter with others to seek an understanding of their situation, it extends to a dialogue with many others whose experiences may have in some way intersected with ours.

I am mindful of the existence of evil in the United States, from the unsolved murder of my wife Fran's daughter Marlys to Hilda's son's murder in the homeless shelter to evils less violent yet just as deadly. But in my experience and for my understanding, there is a difference between evil as I have known it and radical, systemic evil that seeks to deny the very existence of whole portions of humanity. To me, a white male from the United States, radical evil in Central America is like Apartheid in South Africa, while evil in the United States is like the present totally unacceptable racial prejudices in the United States which afflict African Americans. I am told by those who have been to South Africa that it is at least an order of magnitude worse than it is here, even in those parts of Philadelphia which are truly Third World and even for the poorest of the poor.

Life Is A Hard Reality

Radical evil is found in El Salvador, in death squads which terrorize a major part of the population. It is seen in the aftermath of the 1989 election in Nicaragua, particularly as the new government struggles with old problems and new. Poverty and economic hardship continue amid the return of the Contras from Honduras and the wealthy from Miami. The presence of an external source of evil is also acknowledged.

No country in Central America can claim to be free from radical evil and certainly no government of the region can make such a claim. Campesino families live on small farms, but even in the best of conditions, it is not paradise. Though it is usually warm enough that clothing is only needed for modesty, it is often so hot that work is difficult and beyond mere sweat of the brow. There is a continued need for sanitation, education, fertilization, and vaccination, and other means to prevent sickness and hardship.

The temptation to idealize the rural peasant, suggesting that it is somehow a pinnacle of God's glory to be a campesino, is blind idealism. Even under the best of conditions, life is hard and the campesino life span is short. These peasants, living on the small, hot, dry or rain-drenched plot of land which they may not even own, are struggling in the presence of radical systemic evil which is not of their making, as they live close to death.

To cite El Salvador as an example again, the largest single cause of death of those who die under one year of age is diarrhea. A theological inquiry about the sins of babies takes on ironic reality in the death of these infants. Because these deaths can be prevented by the modern technological capabilities we now have, these deaths represent radical evil.

Jon Sobrino has said that theologically, poverty itself is evil. He has said, "Since humanity could solve poverty, therefore poverty is sin. North Americans do not understand poverty, even though there are truly some moving examples of poverty in our country. In Central America, poverty means being very near to death." He noted that few people ever starve to death in Philadelphia, and when they do it is in the newspapers. Professor Sobrino would be the first to acknowledge that his observation concerning Philadelphia is more relevant to the communities he visited when receiving an honorary doctorate at Villanova University in the suburbs of Philadelphia than it was during discussions with a worker at Jeremiah House in North Philadelphia or with Hilda and the other women working with Jobs With Peace.

In San Salvador, it has been said that there is a recent increase in poverty which can be visualized as going from four tortillas per day to two per day, and from one new shirt in a year to none. Then, we were told, when the poor stand up, near death, and say that they want to live, then they are killed.

The campesinos want to have a simple farm, to work the land, find a mate, raise a family and in time die and go to heaven. They do not want, nor do they understand any of the major world forces. Even before Communism's decline, no one seriously argued that the peasant wanted a totalitarian worker state. Capitalism has not reached out to the campesino to offer food, shelter, clothing and health care. Even now, as various factions search for an economic model for El Salvador, the poor only want food.

The campesinos do not want to starve, or be forced off the land by bombs or soldiers or earthquakes. They do not want their children to die, crying and dehydrated, poisoned by the water they crave. Poverty which can be eliminated is radical evil. We ask why the Salvadoran mother does not boil the water as she is told. She says that she herself drinks it and, anyway, it even looks the same after it has been boiled. She asks, "Why don't my neighbors use the latrines my husband helped build?" At least one of her children will probably die of dehydration.

Reality Is Being Hidden

Part of the radical evil we observed is the systemic refusal to even see the poverty. It is possible to travel for days in Guatemala and only see the beauty of the volcanoes and the blue sky and the crops growing up the mountain sides. If one looks a bit closer, one sees colorfully dressed indigenous families in and among the crops and alongside the road. Looking even closer lets one see men and women and children with impossible burdens being carried on their backs and on their heads. Because of cultural training, one can tell the gender of the children by how they carry their burdens. Even at a young age, the males work with their backs, while the women-to-be carry their loads on their heads, to free their hands for the children. The little children carry the babies.

Sometimes one sees a family that is completely involved in the work they do to survive, but sometimes they are together because they have no place to call home. A visit to an orphanage would complete the new vision, to see who is left when someone complains.

In 1991, Guatemala celebrated its first election in which a civilian government turned power over to another civilian government. Democracy was given high praise. Less notoriety was given to the decision by the United States to cut off military aid because of excessive human rights abuses. Not much is said yet about the new president. President Serrano has not yet taken steps to uncover the reality of the power held by the military. One waits for the coup' d'é'tat'.

Nicaragua is not as good at hiding the reality of the suffering of the poor and marginalized. The wealthy are back from Miami in Nicaragua, and clothing styles are changing with fashions. The military dress is less prominent now, as brief cases have replaced AK-47's. The United States dollar buys whatever is needed, if one has dollars. Every street corner has become a variety store, but soon these vendors will be out of inventory as the region's highest cost of living continues to rise.

Sinful reality continues to seek to hide itself, both in individuals and in countries. Jon Sobrino asserted that the path to Development, and the path to Democracy, using both words as defined by the First World, are hiding paths for sin. He suggested that El Salvador is not something that the world wants to acknowledge.

The world does not have an answer. The tragedies of El Salvador are the result of radical, systemic evil in El Salvador, and the world would prefer not to acknowledge it. The world would prefer to keep it hidden.

The death of three United States soldiers in El Salvador at the hands of the guerrillas made headlines, as did the sale of surface-to-air missiles from Nicaragua. The return of the missiles, and for that matter the arrest of the guerillas charged with the killings has not been as well publicized. But those are matters of war. The poverty grinds on in silence except for the screams of its victims.

In Central America, there is sin and poverty, death and alienation, all of the curses of Genesis, Chapter Three. This is overwhelming in El Salvador. In theological terms, the depravity of humanity is in every human, including the campesino and the followers of Sandino and the rich and poor of every country. In terms of religious history, even the Calvinistic description of human depravity, as ponderously evil as that is, is inadequate to explain the radical, systemic evil in Central America.

It Is More Than A Curse

Explanations for this complete pervasiveness of evil can become simplistic. It is easy to say that the life of a peasant is hard, as one would expect. Doesn't Genesis 3:19 say,

In the sweat of your face you shall eat bread until you return to the ground, for out of it you were taken; you are dust, and to dust you shall return.

There is more to the radical, systemic evil that is found in Central America, however, than the life that we all have to live after the Garden of Eden. Most of us work, and work hard. This evil is not that simply explained.

President Duarte of El Salvador told us that "The simplicity of the people (meaning the poor) has prevented change, and the people don't know what democracy is, but they have a feeling that it (democracy) would work under me." The 1988 elections showed a total popular rejection of Duarte's analysis of his society. His party was soundly defeated by the right wing Arena Party and President Alfredo Cristiani. The 1991 elections have shown even more, as many fewer people in El Salvador voted for any candidate. Even the gains by the left are not seen as support for democracy, but rather as a cry for an end to the war.

We have found democracy in El Salvador. But we did not find it there with Mr. Duarte as we met in his Palace. Nor did we find it with Mr. Cristiani as we met him in the Arena Party headquarters, nor even with the Left and Mr. Zamora as we met him in a restaurant.

Democracy exists only in other, hidden places in El Salvador. Democracy, in the form of rule by elected people serving the people they represent, was found in prison, in resettlement camps, in popular church communities and elsewhere with the people who are the poor. These forms of democracy are constantly under attack by the government and the military, with political prison sections broken up, with military invasion of resettlement camps and repatriation settlements, and with kidnapping or murder of leaders from churches when those leaders speak out in defense of the systemic evil. That was all that Archbishop Oscar Romero did. That was all that the Jesuits were doing. That is all that the poor are doing and have been doing all during the civil war.

One compelling story of the attacks on democracy is that of the Independent Human Rights Commission, which had organized a representative government in Mariona Prison. Not long after he was released from prison, the leader, Herbert Anaya was murdered in front of his home. He was shot down as he was taking his children to school. Politicians of one side or another are completely responsible for this crime. Yet the culprits go unpunished.

Years later, Herbert Anaya's family has fled El Salvador and live in exile, and nothing has been done to bring forth justice. Herbert Anaya's wife has ended her tour for support from activists in the United States. She is in another country in Latin America, raising her family and working for peace, justice and human rights while in exile. Her sister works in the northeastern part of the United States with other Salvadoran refugees and with some transformed persons from the United States. There is much work to do.

Radical Evil And The Church

We view the campesino in Central America as one who is beset by evil far beyond the so-called cursed ground and beyond the mere sweat on the brow and beyond the pains of childbirth. The past almost five hundred years have not given much encouragement. Armies and dictators and governments and U.S. Marines and the established church have said the same words to the campesinos. Your suffering is your lot in life. In heaven you will be rewarded. Those words are not words of comfort when they are spoken by those whose every effort is to keep those who suffer from receiving any relief.

We met with a Roman Catholic Bishop in Matagalpa, Nicaragua, who said that he would not talk about politics, but only religious efforts. Bishop Carlos Santi was born in Assisi, Italy, home of the founder of his religious order, and he had been in Nicaragua for more than thirty years. I asked him if it was difficult to minister to those who are released under the amnesty program. He replied, "They worked hard to bring those accused of helping the Contras back into society when the Sandinistas release them."

I said that "I had in mind those who have returned from being with the Contras and want to return to live a normal life." He said that "this was the government's problem, not that of his church." As our procedure on the task force was to listen and not debate with those we saw, I didn't question his pastoral role any further. Still, all our group felt saddened by a policy that divides those who receive pastoral help by what politics one has.

The fact that aid and comfort is rationed, by itself, does not point to or away from any source of the radical evil that is present in the region in Nicaragua. The point that this suggests to me, rather, is that the church has been functioning in Matagalpa in a static, traditional manner, in spite of the transforming presence of a people in need. This is a town where the United States citizen Benjamin Linder is buried, and is a town where widows cry out for help.

Some Sheep, Some Goats

Sadly, that policy and attitude at the top of the Roman Catholic Church in Nicaragua seems to be continuing even now that the war is over and most of the Contra troops are back in Nicaragua. That policy continues in churches throughout all of Central America and throughout all denominations, dividing those who are comforted and those who are not by the political views that they hold. One wonders if the parable of the separation of peoples into sheep and goats at the end times, as told in Matthew 25, should be changed from when the least of these were hungry to "when the least of these had the right political views."

It has been our experience that some change is needed in order to prevent the continuation of systemic evil. In the refusal of some to help, and the refusal of leaders to agitate for change, radical evil is perpetuated. In the same town of Matagalpa, Nicaragua, we spoke with a woman named Christina. She told us that the Contras killed her husband, and that the Sandinistas couldn't or wouldn't help, and the church would not do anything either. She and her four children were victims of radical evil of the type found everywhere in Central America. Neither side in the conflict, nor the church, will help this widow. In her case, she was helping herself in a Habitat For Humanity project that was assisting her to build a house.

I do not want to give the impression that the church is

being singled out as a source of radical evil. Yet the church is not doing nearly enough to be prophetic and to fight effectively against such systemic evil. The churches are often split on the issue of what to do. In El Salvador, we are told that there are two kinds of Baptists. We meet with those who try to help the poor and the widows and the orphans, and we meet with those who have split off from that congregation precisely because it is involved. In Guatemala, we meet Presbyterians who hold meetings to discuss ways to comply with the rules of government. We also meet Presbyterians who seek to help the people in an active but dangerous way. These are but two of many examples.

It unfortunately is not always safe to be active. This became clear to me during one visit I made to Guatemala when I tried to locate a Roman Catholic Brother who was a close friend of one of my friends in Philadelphia. After gaining the confidence of someone who could tell me, I found out that the Brother had left the country after an attempt was made on his life. The church was unable to protect him from being killed if he stayed. In Central America, however, refusing to be pastoral can make one part of the radical evil. Someone must declare that the dictators and the church hierarchy and the military embody a policy that leads to death and destruction. United States policy, in supporting the Salvadoran Army is, as best we can judge from first hand evidence and testimony, supporting raw terrorism and the perpetuation of evil. If the church believes that to be true, how can it not say so? How can the church avoid being a voice of many crying?

Some religious leaders are heard, and some try to be a voice of the voiceless. Sometimes being a voice leads to death. When Archbishop Oscar Romero pleaded with the Army and with the U.S. politicians to stop the killing and to lay down their guns, he was assassinated. When the Jesuits at the University of Central America in San Salvador named the idols of guns and national security, they were assassinated.

Radical evil seems entrenched in Central America. Even the songs that are sung reflect that kind of radical evil. When we were at a refugee camp in El Salvador, in 1986, a song was sung, a song that does not translate nicely into English. I listened, not knowing what was being said until our translator, Jennifer Casolo, asked if I would like to know what was being sung. She was being a voice for these campesinos.

I tried to take notes, and I was in a hurry. I tried for the sense of the song, and filled in the blanks later on the van ride back to the city. Here, I have tried to write the words in some order, and to structure it in hymn form. Listen to these words as I recorded them, with my apology to the composer, the singers and the translator.

> *"The Lord hears the blood of Abel, and the cries of the people awaken Moses.*
> *The scream that is born in our guts they want to silence with 1000 guns.*
> *Misery and hunger, pain and oppression,*
> *put yourself on our side.*
> *We are the oppressed.*
> *The beast tanks squash with hate anyone who gives himself for everyone.*
> *Oh Lord!"*

Radical systemic evil exists in Central America, and the task force experienced it time and again. In the face of such widespread evil, one begins to change from observer to participant. How else can a Christian respond?

4

SUFFERING AND JOY

The second salient feature which I have named and which helps evaluate our experiences is the mixture of suffering and joy. In the presence of all of the radical evil which was experienced in Central America, there is also experienced a unique combination of suffering and joy. This second point, against which the experience of the task force is tested, arises out of the people who have been most strongly affected by the radical evil. Individuals react to the conditions which cause them suffering, and, in the midst of their suffering, they possess a joy. This joy arises from a recognition of the presence of God in their lives as they suffer.

Various denominations have over the years recommended that one day a month be spent fasting and in prayer. For some of us, fasting and prayer has a potential for showing us both suffering and joy, but once again it was a Central American who showed us the way. We were at a retreat center in the fall of 1990, seeking to learn the answer to the question "And Now What?" Much had changed, with elections and changing of power, both in Central America and in the United States. We were gathered to ask that question. At dinner the second night, a Salvadoran man who had been fasting for seven days was sitting with us. We were eating. A Salvadoran woman was reading the Bible to him, talking about Jesus' fast, told in Matthew 4:1-11. There was joy, not pain, as God's word gave meaning to the fast.

The woman reading the Bible to the fasting Salvadoran man was talking to him about Jesus, giving accompaniment to the young man as he fasted. She also knows about "being there" in a time of need. Her brother-in-law was Herbert Anaya, the human rights leader in El Salvador who was assassinated in front of his family as he was taking his children to school. She knew God's presence to be healing and she spoke of that healing often. She offered the fasting man joy with his suffering. Not only was he suffering for his people and for the sake of justice, he presented that suffering to God as the very meaning of his fast was interpreted in the light and guidance of the Bible.

At that meal, we spoke with another Salvadoran man who told us of his father, a journalist, being killed, and of his mother, a high school teacher, being killed, and his sister, a postal worker, being killed, and his twin brother being killed. None were combatants in the war in El Salvador. They were death squad victims. We asked him how he could stand the pain of so many losses. We asked this partly because we have seen an amazing faith in the Salvadoran people, but also because Fran had been helped greatly in her own grief, having had a healing experience with the *Co-Madres*, the Mothers of the Disappeared.

The young man said, "When my brother, my twin brother was killed, every part of me already hurt, and so I could not hurt any more."

We asked, "How did you survive?"

He replied, "I was with others who had suffered, and they helped me know that I was not alone."

That answer was also the experience that Fran had, as she had not totally begun to heal from the murder of her daughter until she, too, had been comforted by others who let her know she was not alone. Knowing that someone is there is such a great help. Of course, knowing that God is there is the ultimate help.

Co-Madres

In San Salvador, not far from the main Roman Catholic Cathedral and the Palace of the Salvadoran Government, a small office on the second floor of a small building houses the work of an organization formed out of the suffering and murders perpetrated by the death squads of the late 1970's and the early 1980's. The Co-Madres, the "mothers of the disappeared", gather here to assist the relatives of the disappeared, those who have been taken from their families.

During the worst times when violent death in San Salvador was so frequent that the death squads were leaving hundreds of their victims in body dumps, mothers and wives organized. They took photographs of the bodies in the body dumps, trying to find a way for the grieving who sought their loved ones to at least identify their sons or their husbands, so that at least the uncertainty would end.

I first visited the office in 1986, and listened to the women tell of the efforts to locate lost or disappeared men and women. Each one had a story, and we listened. We also looked at albums full of photographs of tortured and mutilated bodies. We spoke with the women and we very obviously found a great deal of suffering. Yet we found more. As these women helped each other to look for lost loved ones, some of the pain of their own loss was alleviated in the helping.

At the end of our stay, we had the opportunity to purchase handwork that was for sale to help with the cost of their work. I purchased an embroidery of a scene which included a butterfly, the symbol of hope, for Fran whose daughter Marlys had been murdered in Minnesota in 1979. I told the woman, through an interpreter, I'm sad to say, that I wanted to pay a little extra as a gift because I had a daughter who had been murdered. As those words were translated, the woman became transformed with a look of compassion that I will never forget. She reached out to me with compassion in a way that I cannot over-emphasize.

Reaching Out

Back in the United States, I have spoken of this event often and sometimes those who are listening find tears coming. For me, and for those who were with me and shared it, the experience came close to being in the presence of God. It was an extremely powerful moment. A woman whose whole life was devoted to helping victims of violence had the compassion to reach out to me, in a way that brought joy and comfort to me. Murder had united us.

I have come to understand that Christianity is the source of the capacity these women have to find joy in spite of suffering. The people of Central America stand together in their pain. In being together, at the table fasting, at the cemetery grieving, they know peace. The suffering is still intense and too often leads to death, but the suffering is accompanied by a real and strong Christian faith. That faith finds partnership with God, particularly in the life and death and resurrection of Jesus Christ. For anyone who visits, these mothers of the disappeared become powerful, as Christ was powerful in his humility, even to death on a cross.

In all the suffering that they experience in Central America, the people have a tangible understanding that God is with them in their circumstances. In Nicaragua, at a Habitat for Humanity project on the edge of the Nicaraguan city of Matagalpa, Fran and I spoke with a few of the families who were working on their houses. We played baseball with some of the boys, using a stick for a bat and a rolled up rag for a ball.

A young girl picked a rose and gave it to Fran, and then picked a smaller rose for herself. She said that the small rose was so she would remember her. The girl's father had been murdered.

Faith In God

Perhaps the most powerful example of all of the paradoxical conjoining of suffering and joy of Central America was right there in the barrios and settlements on the edges of ravines in the cities, and in the re-settlements in the countryside. People who owned essentially nothing talked with us, with dignity and honesty. They spoke of their troubles and of their hopes. Their very existence shouted out both suffering and joy.

The encounter that one has with this salient experience, suffering and joy, can be clearly understood as being totally Christian in character. This is not to say that others do not experience suffering or joy or combinations of suffering and joy. Rather, it is to say that the Christian experience is the source of the particular capacity to experience joy with and even in suffering which is encountered in the face of radical evil.

Christianity is a source of their capacity to find joy in suffering because the people of Central America stand together in their suffering. It is in being together that they find joy. It is in living Christianity in a reality that endlessly repeats the life and death of Christ that they find comfort. The suffering is still intense, and leads to death far too often, but the suffering is accompanied by a very real and strong Christian faith. That faith finds partnership with God, particularly in the life and death and resurrection of Jesus Christ. Whatever else is found in Central America, it is not possible to deny the real faith of the people in Jesus

Christ.

In all the suffering that is experienced by the people of Central America, there is a tangible understanding that God is with them in their agony. In Nicaragua, for instance, we met with a widow and her two children. Meylin Castiblanco told us that her husband had been a health worker whose duty was to vaccinate the children of the region where they lived, near the border between Nicaragua and Honduras in the Jinotega Province. He had been trained in Managua and was very proud of his work. Once before, he had been captured by the Contras and told to stop working for the Government. He replied that he was helping the children, not the Government.

Meylin told us how the Contras came to their house and took him by force, at night, while she and the children pleaded for his freedom. He was taken away, and she told us his last words were: "God bless you, and God bless me."

She was sad as any new widow would be, but she talked of his work as being important and how he could not stop helping the children. She wished that her husband was alive; yet she spoke of the lives he saved in his work. Meylin was also able to move past her grief, beyond the bitterness of the conflict. The great tragedy is not that Meylin's husband gave his life for the health of the children, sad as his death was and is for her and their children. The real tragedy, and the shame that falls on everyone, is that the gains of health and life for the children are being lost. The new Nicaragua of returned Contras and of returned refugees from Miami and of unemployed Sandinistas is not even trying to maintain the gains in health care that so many died to bring to the poor. For Meylin and for others who experience joy in suffering, the loss of what had been gained at such a terrible cost is truly a sin.

Sometimes the Christian faith is articulated very clearly, in ways that make the gospel come alive. We had dinner with the medical doctor who was working with the people in the rural area near Matagalpa. During dinner, the doctor told us how one of her nurses had been killed in the mountains as he attempted to vaccinate the children. She could not find anyone who would take his place, and she was not going to stop giving the children the needed care.

This medical doctor told us that she had gone through a phase of being an atheist, but was now finished with that. She told us that she now knows what Jesus meant when he said of his life, "No one takes it from me, but I lay it down of my own accord" [John 10:18]. She said that she walked through the mountains with "a thermos of vaccine over one shoulder and a rifle over the other." What, she asked, did we think of that?"

I have thought a lot about that, as I have tried to understand what is happening in Central America. This doctor is risking her life, and enduring considerable inconvenience at the very least. She is really living the gospel. "The good shepherd lays down his life for the sheep" [John 10:11] has meaning for her as she too is a good shepherd.

Accompaniment

There is throughout Central America a realization of the value of accompaniment, of being there with those who are suffering. In that accompaniment, there is a sharing of the load and of the pain, there is a carrying of one another's burdens, so that somehow the joy that brings survival is present among the people. This may explain why in a Protestant church in San Salvador we heard a pastor say that he and his church leaders were going to attend a rally with the people. He said, "It is better to accompany the people than to give the impression that we have the answers."

The paradoxical combination of suffering and joy is with the people, in El Salvador for example, as poverty forces people to stretch what little they have. Instead of four tortillas per day, now there are only two to eat. In order to win the civil war, the guerillas must destroy the economy, while the Government spends most of the aid the country receives fighting these guerillas and destroying the countryside. Low intensity conflict is draining the life out of the productive parts of the country.

Neither side wants to stop the fighting. Even when accords are reached, other conditions are put forth, to gain more or to prevent having to give what has been won. It has been said of El Salvador that when an outsider looks at this country to see who wants dialogue that will actually end the killing and fighting between the two sides of the civil war, it is hard to find a representative of either side who can seriously say that talks with the other side are even worth attending. The United States Embassy people tell us that the war may last 10 or 15 years, and a Salvadoran General says that they can win the war if they begin to disregard human rights issues.

The recent talks, and the apparent freedom that the United Nations negotiators have to push both sides, does bring some hope. In the dimmer light of the 1990's, out of the world's spotlights but not totally in the shadows of forgottenness, there is change taking place in El Salvador. But the advice is still valid. As we look at this country to see who wants dialogue, we are encouraged by more and more groups and individuals on the sidelines who cry out for dialogue to end the fighting. There is movement and perhaps it will bring peace at last.

Our homeless delegation found one instance when we felt that the Salvadoran Army let us accomplish our small goal because we had come in the face of the death of the Jesuits and their co-workers. We hadn't been deterred, and how can we be stopped if we aren't afraid of death? That is a question we will come back to again several times.

Jon Sobrino suggests that the first world does not want to acknowledge the existence of the real El Salvador. He points to the lack of news reports in the United States press and the unwillingness of people to listen to those who have visited the country. The first world does not have an answer to the problems of sin and poverty, and El Salvador is the result of this lack of answers. What is truly confusing to the first world is the existence of hope in the people.

Hope: Fragile And Absurd

It is absurd to have hope in El Salvador, says Professor Sobrino, but it is real and it exists. It is also fragile. In the time between my first visit in November 1986 and a second visit in January 1988, Professor Sobrino's view of hope changed a bit. Hope arose in the face of the absurd by the people using reality as their theological argument. As time has passed this hope has become the hope to survive one more day. After the murder of his fellow Jesuits, Sobrino did not abandon hope; rather he sought solidarity with the poor who had so many die. In commemorating the martyrdom of those well known, the martyrdom of the many is also being lifted up for the world to see. Hope, fragile and absurd, still flowers.

The people of El Salvador have come together in a community of Tres Ceibas, in a resettlement, which cannot be reached by bus. For the poor, this means that they must spend several hours walking to bring in food and supplies from the nearest town that has supplies. On her first visit to Tres Ceibas, my wife Fran saw twin boys, eight days old. The mother was nursing one boy, but she only had milk for one. The father was feeding the other little baby sugar water, and the family was waiting for the end. The delegation Fran was with gave some money to the church for milk and other supplements.

The community has survived nearby fighting, even through the major offensive of 1989, and it has struggled to survive against war and isolation. The fact that it still exists is a victory. The families struggle, and yet there is growth and growth means life. Both parents still hold the twins, but now with joy. This is the experience of visiting Central America that shapes and transforms those of us who visit the region, as we experience the suffering and the joy.

Both Fran and I visited Tres Ceibas again to see the twin boys and to find the wonderful surprise that Maria and Antonio had once again delivered twins, this time a boy and a girl. This time, also, the community store room had a good supply of powdered milk. This time there was joy in the celebration of the birth, because there was hope that basic food would continue to be available.

It Is Still Hope

Professor Sobrino is clearly a man who understands and who loves the people of El Salvador. He told us that they are not sad. They may be tired or angry at something, but to live makes sense. To live makes such sense that in their scarred lives the people are happy. They have found a hidden treasure, which is the feeling that they belong to real humanity. They do not live in the unreal, but have the roots of their dignity in their humanity. Suffering dignifies their humanness.

Some who live this way stand out, like Archbishop Oscar Romero did, and some of the priests and pastors and campesinos do as they seek to live the gospel of Jesus Christ in El Salvador. Mostly, however, the ones who experience suffering and in that suffering find joy are the ordinary people.

If there is an answer, it is to be found with these people, the poor of El Salvador. It is the people of this group, with all their imperfections and with all their human failings, who are the real reality of El Salvador. Because the poverty is so great and because poverty in El Salvador means that one is on the edge of death, this struggle of the poor is in reality the struggle of the cosmos between good and evil, between life and death. All those who oppose the life of the poor are opposing goodness and wittingly or unwittingly align themselves on the side of evil and of death. This alignment with evil has been made clear to those of us who have changed from observer to participant.

Evil exists in Central America in tangible form that is recognizable. It is not merely the imperfection of humanity seeking to live in the world. The smiles on the faces of the people in spite of this very visible evil are the smiles of those who have chosen life. In the suffering of the people is a joy of being alive, and a joy of life itself. It is the joy of creation.

Ordinary Life And Death

In 1988, we met the Bishop of the Lutheran Church in El Salvador, Bishop Medardo Gomez, in his home. It is a modest home, with sleeping rooms in the back part of the house. There is a television, and we gathered around that to view a 15 minute video produced by a branch of the Lutheran Church located in the United States. The video spoke of the life and work of this Bishop, and of the death threats and tragedy that are a daily part of that life and work.

After the video, we sat in a large roofless room near the front door, talking and listening to Bishop Gomez and to his wife. He graciously spoke to us of his efforts to follow the teachings of Christ. He talked about being threatened, and about being betrayed. It would be easy, he shared, to leave for the security of another country. During the worst of the fighting in 1989, he and his family did take refuge outside of El Salvador. He said, "It is easy to leave for security, but our brothers and sisters are here.It is better to struggle together. Here I stand." He spoke, adding to the words of Martin Luther, "Here I stand with you. You are not alone. The Lord is with us."

Bishop Gomez spoke the words of a prophet. "The reality of El Salvador is one of death. The Lutheran Church [of El Salvador] tries to be the history of life in the reality of death. It tries to be a contradiction to the force of death, because death has been installed as the power and life is trying to emerge."

The church," he said, "is testimony inspired by faith." But faith alone is not enough. Bishop Gomez continued, "The pilot prays when he gets into his airplane to drop bombs. Some seek to end the war by a total war, done in the name of God. Genocide is here, being done as a political act." Then he asked, "What is the response? The struggle is between life and death, and it is the Spirit of God that guides us."

Bishop Medardo Gomez also has an adopted daughter. He and his wife found her the day she was orphaned by the war three days after her birth. She has been with them ever since, and her name is Fey y Esperanza, [Faith and Hope.] She is the little queen of that household, and brings joy to everyone who visits.

Only A Priestly Role

The role of the church is clearly important to bring about a viable option for the poor, trying to create a sanctuary from the fighting, as a model for the country. Yet the church was unable to protect Bishop Gomez and other priests and pastors and Christian workers. The martyred Jesuits are visible examples of the death that is dealt to so many who are not so famous. Events keep showing that the church does not have the force to withstand or prevent the radical evil that is rampant in Central America.

We have learned that in El Salvador, for example, the "church" is doing some very nice things. It is working very hard to help the people who have struggled to have resettlement of their homeland. The events after the signing of the Arias Peace Plan, allowed many refugees to return to El

Salvador from Honduras. The church has been helpful in seeing that food got through to the resettlement camps. The church generally denounced the wrongs by all sides in the conflict. Yet the church has not speak prophetically.

There is a campaign known in the United States as the "Going Home" campaign, and much money and supplies have raised as most of the Salvadoran refugees who had fled to other Central American countries did go home. And they stayed home. Repatriation and repopulation are movements that have flowered out of the solidarity of the people and grown strong with the accompaniment of internationals.

We look for a prophet of God to say with strength and authority: *"This is what the Lord says. Stop the war."* The surprise amid all the suffering and joy is that it is the *people* who tell us to stop the war, and the *people* tell visitors from the United States to stop the war.

Archbishop Oscar Romero was assassinated in El Salvador on March 24, 1980. He was a prophet who cried out that the war must stop. He also said that if he was killed because he spoke out for the people, he would rise up again in the people. There is much suffering in El Salvador, but there is joy in the people, as though there is a prophet among them. Some think that Archbishop Romero has risen up again in the people. God is present, that is certain.

The Lutheran Church and Bishop Medardo Gomez have been threatened for their work to help the poor. Bishop Gomez told us that the work of Roman Catholic Archbishop Romero was work which was filled with the Holy Spirit. Bishop Gomez said that perhaps those who attacked and killed Romero may have in fact committed the unpardonable sin of an assault on the Holy Spirit. Medardo Gomez may be the next prophet of El Salvador if he is allowed to live that long. Even now he brings joy to those who suffer.

There is much suffering in all of the countries of Central America, of course. And there is joy among the sufferers, and there is joy amidst the suffering. All are seeking a prophet to

lead them, and to stop the suffering. People everywhere turn
to the Bible for comfort, seeking a prophet. A minister who
has worked in Central America tells of his trials and pain as
he sees the suffering of the people. He says that as he goes
walking, to be with God and to have his own time, he
sometimes recites these words:

> *"He gave me beauty for ashes,*
> *the oil of joy for mourning,*
> *A garment of praise*
> *for the spirit of heaviness.*
> *I am a tree of righteousness, a planting of the Lord,*
> *That He might be glorified."*

Those words are prophetic, taken from verse three of
Isaiah, Chapter 61. The first two verses, which St. Luke tells
us Jesus recited in his home church/synagogue, preaching the
good news and setting free the captives, are used by many to
proclaim the liberation of the people of Central America. Yet
the third verse, with its comfort, permitted our group of
United States visitors to see some of the joy of the prophet's
message. We were to experience joy amidst the suffering.

This is the message that we bring home. Amidst the
radical evil of Central America, there is both suffering and
joy. These experiences transform visitors from the United
States from observers to participants. We returned and began
our dialogue with our own denomination and with the larger
church at home and in the rest of the world.

5

DIALOGUE WITH THE LARGER CHURCH

The church in Central America has been part of the radical evil and the suffering and joy in Central America since the earliest days of the Spanish conquest. The first Roman Catholic Bishop of Central America, Bishop Francisco Maroquin, installed the alliance between the church and the conquistadores in Guatemala in 1537. The first Roman Catholic Bishop to be martyred for the poor, Bishop Antonio Valdivieso, died trying to change those alliances in Nicaragua on February 26, 1550.

Our experiences as Christians have been shaped by the events like these in Central America, including the actions of the church which is a very real part of the radical evil in some cases and is a very real part of the suffering and joy in other cases. The church in Central America is built on centuries of both suffering and joy and of radical and systemic evil.

Also, it should be quite obvious that we are shaped by our experiences in dialogue with the larger church. Beginning with our own denomination and extending outward to other denominations in the United States, both Protestant and Catholic, and then to other churches in North and South America, in Europe, and elsewhere, we have had a dialogue with the larger church.

How Do We Speak?

This third salient point, dialogue with the larger church, has had a major impact on whole congregations, dioceses, and even denominations. Much could be said about having ears to hear and eyes to see. It is hard to have dialogue with anyone who will not listen. As has been explained earlier, some people do not want to hear what is being said, and do not want to understand what those who have been there have observed. The transformation from observer to participant is not pleasant, and it is not made easier by hearing the experiences second hand.

This difficulty was one we have discussed often. One particular night very late in Managua, Nicaragua, I was in a conversation with someone who had been to Honduras but not to El Salvador. I thought it was clear that the church in El Salvador had no prophet at that time. He responded, saying that this was true in Honduras also. "But remember," he said, "the church is not the prophet. The church awaits the prophet".

If this is true, we must be aware of the real temptation to regard our words as the words of the prophets of today, especially when entering into dialogue with the larger church. We do not want to claim to be more than we are. We understand that what we say and what we write is done with the full knowledge that we see imperfectly, hear less than what is said and sometimes do not hear what is said. Though we are transformed from observers to participants, we speak out of that transformation made in the presence of radical evil, tempered with suffering and joy.

I truly believe that we experience the presence of the divine, but we have no more claim on freedom from radical evil than anyone else. It is essential to remember that we speak to the larger church. We speak to and not for a particular church or a specific denomination. In that way we are like the prophets who spoke to the people of God. Yet we must be mindful of the humanity and failings of those who were prophets of God. We must testify to what has been written on our heart, to say, this is what we have seen and we are speaking for those who have no voice to speak. We speak for those who are crying and there are many.

And if, when we speak, we have had an incarnational experience, one that has changed us and given us new life, we speak with the conviction which comes from that experience. But also, as did the prophets of Israel, we speak to those who would listen. We bring a message from those who have no voice to speak. As voices of the many crying in the wilderness, we are true to our promise to tell what we heard and saw, so that others may have the opportunity to see and hear as well. Is prophecy more than that?

This Is Where It Started

Sometimes, it seems, one is thrust into a position of controversy not unlike that faced by the prophets of old. This happened to me as I returned from my first trip to Central America. The very next day, on Sunday, I preached a sermon. I am not sure the congregation was ready for me, and I am not sure I was ready for them. I started by saying that I spoke to them, to the church, not for the denomination or anyone other than myself. I couldn't even speak for the others who were with me, as we had not yet completed our report. But as I spoke, there was total attention. One could hear a pin drop.

During the sermon, I spoke about missing my family. I said that I missed them all, but most of all I missed my 15 year old son because I saw so many young boys in uniform, with guns and grenades and weapons provided by the United States. I said I wanted to tell these 14 and 15 year old boy soldiers about my son and his school activities and his Christian clowning. I wanted to tell them about the other 15 year old boys who I knew, and wrestling teams and youth groups and pizza. I wanted to talk to these young soldiers about a life they had no chance to have, but, of course, I could not.

The United States Government policy has for years been based upon obtaining a military solution in El Salvador. The United States Government policy was based upon obtaining a military solution in Nicaragua, where Contra Aid was substituted for direct talks of peace. How could I tell these young men/boys that we sent guns so that they could kill or be killed in implementing our government's policies? How, I asked, can one talk to young boys who are to kill or be killed to carry out policy. At that time, I spoke about a United States policy in Central America which was based upon a military victory, not a negotiated peace. Surrender was the only option offered then.

Later I was told that I had upset a friend of mine, who told others that we had to fight communism in Central America so that my son and the others could continue their American life for which we had fought. Other young men from our country died for this freedom. Does that "American life" have to include inflicting violence and terror on the poorest people of Central America? How is he so sure it is really communism that is being fought? Is it not possible that violence and terror actually encourage communism? He does not talk to me anymore.

That sermon was the beginning of my own dialogue with the larger church. After the sermon, during the time to have fellowship, the questions started. As a person transformed from observer to participant, as a person confronted by radical evil, as a person participating in suffering and joy, I began a dialogue which continues to this day.

I had been warned of what to expect. In Matagalpa, we had met with Mrs. Gladys Bob, the widow of a coffee grower. Her husband had been killed by the Contras and she was carrying on the family business. She had been to the United States, as part of her efforts to find a market for her coffee, and she had been in dialogue with the North American public. She told us that as a Nicaraguan she faced three questions over and over, as she spoke with the people of the United States. In her experience, these three questions are: What about communism in Nicaragua? What about "free press"? What about religious freedom?

I found quite quickly that these three questions dominated the discussions I had with people at home, even if I made a point of addressing these issues in my presentation. If I spoke about communism in one form, such as Marxist analysis of land ownership, I was asked about Cuban or Soviet advisors. If I spoke about Cuban or Soviet hospitals and doctors, I was asked about collective farms. Similarly, the freedom of press and freedom of religion and religious worship were always brought into the conversation. I was not surprised when these three questions were asked in the White House by President Ronald Reagan.

It Is Not Only Political

There are others who listen to sermons and lectures, and admit that what I have experienced is valid and true, at least within the range of my experiences. They say, however, that it is political and has no place in church. I respond by saying that my message and the message of others like me are not solely political, and that what we say can't be dismissed for including the political when it encompasses so much more. The message calls us to understand that God is with the poor in their suffering and joy, under the threat of radical evil.

Sometimes I tell these people about Bishop Desmond

Tutu's statement that "If you are neutral in a situation of injustice, you have chosen the side of the oppressor. If an elephant has his foot on the tail of a mouse, and you say you are neutral, the mouse will not appreciate your neutrality."

If the biblical message is internalized and if political issues are kept out of its life, then the church fails to live up to the responsibility it has been given. That responsibility is to await the prophets and to prepare the people for Christ, and how the church responds to that responsibility will be judged as in Matthew 25. Churches too will be separated into the sheep and the goats.

I understand that the responsibility of the church and an essential part of its mission is to respond to the conditions of the people of the world. If that response includes a statement on a political issue, the response must still be made, whether it be in El Salvador or in Nicaragua or in the United States. The poor in Central America are a responsibility of the church, because the church has been at least partly responsible for the conditions that caused them to be poor. The church must go beyond political issues to help the poor to change these conditions.

I have been asked in these conversations what happens to the poor when they are liberated. This is a basic question that all of us ask as we begin to examine "liberation" theology. I answer that the 'liberated poor' accompany those who are still poor, just as we are called to do. Sometimes this question reveals an elitist mentality, asking if we can trust the poor to govern properly. I try to explain that dirty and uneducated people can be emancipated, particularly when we really don't have all the answers in our cleaner, more educated lives. How can we say we are different in God's eyes? Only God as parent has all the answers, and if that seems simplistic, it is because our faith asks us to understand just that. Love God and love our neighbor, and leave parenting to God.

In this dialogue with those in the larger church who

really are concerned, we learn that accompaniment may be the appropriate response to those who are oppressed. This is the response of those who have been transformed from observer to participant. This is the reason why anyone who has gone to Central America seeks out others who have more recent news. This is the reason why we return to Central America to be with the people, to again be in accompaniment with their suffering and joys and to be part of their hope.

Nor Is It Conservative

There has been considerable criticism of the work of Central American activists by those who represent more conservative parts of the various churches. In the first issue of the *Presbyterian Layman* newspaper which was published after some of us visited with President Ronald Reagan and other top government leaders, for example, the President of the Presbyterian Lay Committee, Robert Campbell, published an open letter to President Reagan. In that letter, Campbell said that Mr. Reagan should be aware that there is another point of view in this denomination. I called Mr. Campbell after that column, and we had lunch. He had suggested that there was another side to what we had seen, and I asked to see that side.

We had a good exchange at lunch, and he loaned me his file. There was a lot more to the conversation than this, of course, but his main objection was not the findings of the task force. His main objection was that there were few, if any, really conservative members appointed.

I told him that it didn't matter who was appointed. I told him also that the experience was transforming, and that he should go with me on a delegation Fran and I were organizing.

As it turned out, he could not go, but his aide did go with us to Guatemala and to Nicaragua. We returned from that trip just before the extremely close, politically embroiled vote in the United States Congress on Contra funding. Essentially all of the politically conservative Members of Congress voted for Contra Aid. Speaking unofficially in my home church, the conservative young man who had traveled with us described his transformation from observer to participant, and suggested that we cannot pray enough. He said that he too was now opposed to military aid to the Contras. He had experienced a change of heart like many others , and his change of heart is just one more example of my belief that every Christian who really visits the region comes back to tell the same story.

Now, nearly four years later, I wish I could take some of the writers for the *Presbyterian Layman* newspaper with me on a delegation to Nicaragua, particularly. We have been in conversation, trying to temper their use of labels for the activities of those who work in Nicaragua and who support the work of these Christians. We have not been able to have this mission work characterized as Christian without additionally having an ideological spin placed on the work.

When we dialogue with the larger church, when we get the opportunity to join together in fellowship becoming transformed from observer to participant, we are Christian, not political. It is not a question of being conservative or liberal. The key is in the dialogue, and not in the point of view from which the dialogue is begun. And since it is a dialogue, it never ends.

A Mass With 17 Bishops

On the first anniversary of the murder of the Jesuits and their staff at the University of Central America in San Salvador, a mass was said. There were 17 bishops in attendance, and more than 100 priests. The text of the message, written on a banner and read during the mass, was from the Apocalypse, or the Book of Revelation 6:9-10,

When he opened the fifth seal, I saw under the altar the souls of those who had been slain for the word of God and for the witness they had borne; they cried out with a loud voice, "O Sovereign Lord, holy and true, how long before thou wilt judge and avenge our blood on those who dwell upon the earth?"

There were some who had been at the funeral mass one year before, where so many church people had said so many words. They wondered if once again a child would lead them. At that funeral mass in 1989, a young girl had been given a chance to speak, and her words were the words that were remembered. That day she was the voice of the many crying, as she said, "Don't weep for them. Imitate them!"

Some of those who were there with us had also attended the funeral mass in 1980, when Archbishop Oscar Romero was buried. They reminded us of the shooting and bombs fired by the Salvadoran Army that led to the deaths of those who sought to be part of that mass. We wondered if that would be true here, as helicopters flew over the campus from time to time.

We wondered if there would be guns and death, or would there be words and life. It was a time of anxiety that ended with a most memorable symbolism, rather than guns or words. For us, the presence of God was not in the music or the preaching or the eulogy. Rather, a family member of each person who had been murdered walked across the platform and received a small jar containing soil which had been taken from the grounds and which contained the very blood of the women and the Jesuits. One could almost hear God.

And the Lord said, "What have you done? The voice of your brother's blood is crying to me from the ground."

At the mass, I felt so sad when I saw the Archbishop as he and the procession of clergy entered. I felt overwhelmed with the inability to bring peace to a land that cried out. This mass should not have to be. The Jesuits should be teaching, not in tombs. The two women should be with their family, not just in their memories. There was no magic moment, only the reality of death.

I remembered Archbishop Oscar Romero. That martyred saint has become a symbol of the struggle for life over death and of good over evil. I remembered the movie *ROMERO* and the scene where Monsignor Romero confronts the priest who has taken up a gun. In the movie, the priest shouted his question, "What other answer is there?" and Monsignor Romero answered, "I don't know but if you take the gun you will be just like them." How absolutely correct was that observation by Monsignor Romero. Violence in El Salvador causes the very ground to cry out to the Lord.

That was the dialogue with the larger church. Take up the gun and you will be just like them. And who are they? They are those who solve problems with guns and violence, and who reject words and dialogue. And it is for that reason that our dialogue with the larger church continues and it is why our dialogue seems to some to be political. As a voice of many crying, we ask that the guns be put down. Our understanding of God with us, in the incarnational experiences we have, leads us to accompaniment, to "imitate them", and to cry out, "What have you done?"

A Lesson Learned

The next day, after the mass with the 17 bishops and more than 100 priests, we participated in a meeting of Salvadoran and North American activists who came together to review the situation and to make plans to move ahead in efforts to bring peace and justice to El Salvador. We were to use words, not guns.

This day was not my best day in Central America, but rather was about one of the worst days I have had in the region. It is worthy to note that transformed participants have bad days too. I was fighting something, both stomach and fever. I wanted to go home. I didn't like grey iron bars and beds that stink and not being able to sleep. I do not like not having a pillow. I don't like cold showers. I don't like mosquitoes. And, I was aware that I needed to know the answer to a question I wrote in my notebook. "What is going on, as we preach one thing and do another?"

As we met, we heard various speakers discuss various points of view. Once again, I heard, "I am sure of one thing (concerning the murders of the Jesuits and the women) and that is that the U.S. Embassy is covering up something and that is a crime." Once again, radical, systemic evil was present.

There was hope expressed as well. We who were from the north were thanked for our support. Cheers went up. Que Viva! For solidarity! At these kinds of events, in the true spirit of democracy, everyone has a chance to speak. For some, this was both suffering and joy.

I had an opportunity to bring words from the homeless delegation, after consultation with my friends. We were reflecting on the concept of "the church" and the proposition that "The church that proclaims conversion in the midst of war seeks to assure peace with social justice." This was the theme of the meeting.

The response of the Philadelphia homeless delegation began with a reading from the Apocalypse, or the Book of Revelation 3:7-8,

> And to the angel of the church in Philadelphia write: 'The words of the holy one, the true one, who has the key of David, who opens and no one shall shut, who shuts and no one opens.
>
> "'I know your works. Behold, I have set before you an open door, which no one is able to shut; I know that you have but little power, and yet you

have kept my word and have not denied my name. '"

My remarks opened with the question of whether or not
the church of Philadelphia was willing to go through that
open door? I recalled my first trip and my reading of the
Gospel of Mark, just after John the Baptist was murdered, and
the first words of Jesus. *"Repent for the kingdom of God is at
hand."* We had been focusing on the church as it proclaims
conversion and on repenting, *cambien su vida,* because in fact
the kingdom of God was at hand. It is proper to focus on
conversion, but it is also proper to focus on the kingdom of God.

As the Gospel of Mark does after those first words of
Jesus, we look at the life and the death of Jesus. We look at
the incarnation, that of God in human form. I said that I was
reminded of the words of Padre Jon de Cortina, who said, "If
God is not with the poor of El Salvador, then God is
nowhere." We who have been transformed from observer to
participant have seen God. We believe in God. Who else
carries us as we struggle in the valley of the shadow of
death?

For that reason, we say that if God is somewhere, God
is with the poor who suffer! God is with the suffering poor.
God is with the martyrs whose death we honored that week
in El Salvador. And, if God is with those who suffer, it is
truly an incarnation. Jesus went to the Father so that he
would send the mighty Comforter. The Holy Spirit is sent by
the Father to us here and now.

I told the group about our delegation which had two
women whose children were murdered, one in her home and
the other in a homeless shelter. I told about how these
women reached out to a newly bereaved woman in the village
of Santa Cruz, in Usulatan Province.

I talked about the others from Philadelphia. One of
our delegation, a woman, was a former Black Panther who
had renounced violence as a means to an end. Our delegation
had two men who had dedicated their lives to anti-war work

in the United States, and they marched with banners calling for the war to stop in El Salvador. Two others of our men had been arrested in El Salvador and Honduras for their accompaniment of the refugees coming home to El Salvador.

The church is not the kingdom of God, but the church must point to the kingdom of God. The church in Philadelphia cannot wash its hands of the death of the martyred Jesuits and women, like Pilate washed his hands of the death of Jesus. The church in Philadelphia must join with the churches in El Salvador to proclaim the kingdom.

A Most Clear Statement

Richard Withers, a carpenter and lay monk with our delegation said, "If we are not one of those who are persecuted and if we wish to participate in the kingdom, we must be in physical solidarity with those who are persecuted, even unto death." Richard's understanding is the most clear statement of accompaniment that I have heard. If we seek to enter the kingdom of God and are not ourselves persecuted, we must be in physical solidarity with those who are.

This was the model of Monsignor Romero and the Jesuit martyrs. More than that, it is the model of Jesus Christ. I closed my talk by saying that we must work together to assure peace with justice, even at the cost of our lives. That was nearly a prophetic description of events that would take place the next day.

So, if we reflect on the church that preaches conversion in the midst of war, we must assure peace with social justice, even at the cost of our lives. And if this is what we preach, we cannot let our actions be otherwise. That is the message we must tell the larger church. Not only must we point to the kingdom of God, we must also lead the way. To do otherwise would be to deny the name of Jesus.

This third salient point, dialogue with the larger

church, has, therefore, caused an interaction with many
congregations across this country. It has also caused those of
us who would be a voice of many crying to experience a fourth
major experience. This experience is our dialogue with
government.

6

DIALOGUE WITH THE GOVERNMENT

My own experience in dialogue with the government took its most significant step when I joined six other Presbyterians at the White House for a meeting with President Ronald Reagan and other top administration officials. The invitation, which I never even dreamed would happen, came at just the right time. Late one night in July, 1987, Fran and I were sitting on our porch, enjoying the summer warmth and talking about the state of our efforts in Central America.

I had been leading a week of talks at a church, trying to have a dialogue. Attendance was poor. We were feeling shunned by some in the congregation and others were open in disbelief. To some, our patriotism was questionable. We were suffering as a result of our encounter with radical evil in Central America, and had found no joy in our dialogue with the larger church. I was as depressed as I have been about Central America. I was at the emotional bottom. The phone rang, and I did not expect good news. Who calls with joy late at night?

The phone call was from a secretary in the office where I work part time. She is the most reliable worker in the office, and never puts things off. This night, however, she had just remembered that she had taken a call at the office for me, from California, from a Presbyterian Church secretary, who wanted to know if I would be able to go to the White House in August to discuss the 1987 Task Force report.

President Reagan had been given a copy of the report by the man he calls pastor, the Reverend Donn Moomaw. Moomaw had sent the report with a short cover note. Reagan and others in the White House had read the task force report after it was adopted by the 1987 General Assembly. Reagan had asked Moomaw, his pastor, "How can this be?" After some discussion in which our previous briefings by the State Department were explained, an invitation was given to the Reverend Gary Demarest, another California Presbyterian minister and a member of the task force, to select and invite part of the task force to the White House.

In The White House

Initially, after clearing White House security, we met with Frank Carlucci, then the National Security Adviser, and several aides including General Colin Powell. The dialogue was honest. Carlucci said he took issue with some of our conclusions. For example, he said, he objected to our statement that there was no democracy in El Salvador. He mentioned elections. I responded respectfully that I had been a lawyer too long to believe that the power to use confessions obtained by torture was part of democracy. Torture and other human rights violations weren't part of United States democracy and we should expect no less from El Salvador.

After this dialogue, we were taken to the Roosevelt Room, where we met Secretary of State George Schultz, Vice President George Bush, and others on the staff. Reagan entered, spoke momentarily with each of us while the photographer took pictures. Then we all took our assigned places at the conference table and Pastor Moomaw introduced the group and led us in prayer.

Reagan opened with prepared remarks, using note cards. Schultz then added additional background and policy remarks which were exclusively in east-west terms. Demarest spoke for our group, focusing on the issue of religious freedom in Nicaragua and suggesting that our denomination stood ready to help bring about peace.

After remarks by Reagan about the Miskito Indian relations in Nicaragua, I spoke, reaffirming our desire and ability to help. I cited the work of the Moravian Church in bringing about peace between the Nicaraguan government and the Miskito, Rama, Sumo and other Atlantic Coast groups. I said that our denomination had close relations with the Moravian Church and that we could do much to bring people together. The Moravians had not taken sides, but had sought to bring peace through dialogue. That was what we wanted to do as well.

Each of the others on the task force then spoke about what was most important for him or her to say. Each of us was articulate and showed respect for the office and the man, President Ronald Reagan. Reagan later shared with Moomaw in a letter after the visit that he "appreciated the good discussion we had." We did too.

Rendering To Caesar

Since the meeting with the President of the United States, I have spent a lot of time thinking about the dialogue and trying to see the event in humanitarian and theological terms rather than in ideological stereotypes. For quite some time afterward, I could not stop thinking of things that I could have said but didn't, yet each new thought somehow faded as I began to understand that each of us heard and said what was appropriate at the time. A dialogue took place at several levels of communication.

On the surface, however, the dialogue was clearly concerned with the issue of who should determine the existence of religious freedom in Nicaragua. Although our report deals with other issues and other countries at length, this issue was primary in the conversation. Does the state or the church decide if Nicaragua has religious freedom? Once the decision is made between church and state, one can argue that it should be Republican or Democrat, Presbyterian or Roman Catholic, but these are secondary issues.

Our visit and the words we spoke said that the church should decide for itself whether it has religious freedom. The church should never surrender the right to make that decision. The Bible is full of examples where the people of God tried to rely on themselves rather than on God, on the state rather than the church. Religious freedom is not something one renders to Caesar.

I don't think that our church leaders pay enough attention to this clear distinction between what is Caesar's and what belongs to God. I don't think that the mild protests of the church are ever going to keep this distinction clear, that the church does not serve God when the church gives up the right to determine what belongs to God. Certainly, when Caesar claims to know what a just war is, the church should stand up and be prophetic. Caesar is not known for the truth.

Beneath the surface of the dialogue was the issue of truth. Church people have studied, have prayed, have reflected and have reached certain conclusions. The denomination has accepted those conclusions by adopting the reports. All of the polity of the church was employed, decently and in order, resulting in documents that speak to the members and others who would listen.

Those of us who were invited to meet President Reagan presented to him the truth that we found. We don't know why he wanted us to visit. He didn't ask us to do anything;

he didn't say, "I am your president, do this for me." He didn't tell us why he invited us and, of course, we cannot presume to read his mind. Regardless of the reason, however, I have felt that the President may have been testing our truth. He told us we didn't have access to all the information that exists, and that is true. He told us that there is much disinformation being given in and about Nicaragua, and that is true. Truth does not only belong to the state, however, and truth must also be rendered to God.

At this point, several of us later remarked, we wanted to at least comment on what we had found was massive disinformation by the United States government concerning events in Central America, particularly in Nicaragua. But that was not our purpose in meeting with the President. In spite of the blatant disinformation campaign by some in the Administration, we were not present to confront but to bring an offer to work for peace.

It takes faith to reach out for peace, and it takes great faith to reach out for peace in an entire region. It was only 5 days after the Arias plan had been signed in Guatemala City, and there was hope for peace. And so we offered to help. Each of us offered to help and to use our contacts to bring about peace.

What Was Accomplished?

Friends have asked me why we didn't say this or that, why we didn't challenge what was said. I know why I didn't say anything to cause a confrontation. We as individuals and as representatives of the church are ready to bring about a just peace. The one thing we wanted to leave with Mr. Reagan and his staff was an understanding of our sincere desire to assist in that process.

Afterward, when we talked about our encounter, we found that this unspoken goal was in all of our minds, that we demonstrated our desire to help bring peace.

Ultimately, the dialogue became an act of faith. As Bonhoeffer wrote in *The Cost of Discipleship*, "to resist the power [that actually exists] is to resist the ordinances of God, who has so ordered life that the world exercises dominion by force and Christ and Christians conquer by service." Each member of the task force willingly became vulnerable and by refusing to have a confrontation, we submitted as Christians. Religious freedom is not something one renders to Caesar, nor is truth, for truth opposes radical evil. By being vulnerable and open, we placed the ultimate outcome of our concern in God's hands. God is the one who has the power to decide.

We are asked, "What did you accomplish by the visit?" If we place our faith in God, we accomplished much. We are still facing toward God in prayer. During the time of the second task force trip, in January, 1988, we followed practically on the footsteps of some of the administration officials we met as they toured the Central American countries in preparation for the next meeting between the presidents of those countries. We do not have access to precise information on the efforts of Elliot Abrams and Colin Powell to overthrow the Nicaraguan Government, but we have heard their support of the Contras and their condemnation of the Nicaraguan government when the Sandinistas were in power.

From August, the time of the Arias plan and our visit to the White House, to January and the talks in Costa Rica, somehow peace had survived. We don't take credit for the peace efforts, nor do we actually think our words had any major effect. Still, we can't be sure. Our obligation was to speak out then and we did. We have continued to speak.

It was not until just before this book went to print that I learned that the Contra leaders were in the White House with President Reagan and these same members of the Administration on August 4, 1987, just 3 days before the Arias Peace Plan was signed and 8 days before our visit. I mention this visit by the Contra leaders to the White House for two reasons.

First, as a digression, I learned this information from Steven Kinser's book, *BLOOD OF BROTHERS*, G.P. Putnam's Sons, New York, 1991, and I want to say a few things about that book. I offer this as my own opinions, not as an expert in Central America anywhere near Mr. Kinser's experience, but as one who has had a different experience than he. His book is worth reading, in order to have a more complete background on Nicaragua, where he was bureau chief for the New York Times. It is a compendium of all sorts of facts and rumors, impressions and prejudices, opinions and observations. One who reads *BLOOD OF BROTHERS* should already be very high on the Central America learning curve so they will be able to distinguish each of the compendium from all of the others.

Our Primary Statement

The second reason for mentioning the visit by the Contra leaders to the White House at that time was that our primary statement to the Reagan Administration and to Mr. Reagan, was that we hoped that he and they would invite representatives of the Nicaraguan church to speak as we had done. We were, at most, representatives of the church in the United States, using a loose definition of representation, since we were only invited on the suggestion of one or two members of one denomination. We certainly did not presume to speak for the larger church, but only from our own perspectives. Still, we were invited, I think, because we represented the part of the church in the United States which did not agree with the Administration.

The only persons with both the authority and the knowledge to speak of the atrocities and inhumanities of the Contra campaign would have been the church leaders who were given the pastoral responsibility to minister to the victims of the Contra campaign. Only the Nicaraguan church could really tell the story of their ministry and the violence being done to the civilian population by the Contras. They could and would speak to violence by the Sandinistas as well. There was a time when we were meeting with Mr. Reagan that he used the words "freedom fighters." We all let that pass as that had been his term for the Contras for some time. However, I had been tempted to suggest that George Washington would turn over in his grave if he thought that persons killing nurses and pregnant women were equated with his soldiers at Valley Forge. Perhaps that would have been the patriotic thing to say in defense of the reputation of those who won freedom for the United States. But I didn't say what I thought because I wanted to avoid confrontation over labels in the hope that the church leaders of Nicaragua would have a chance to tell their story.

A Story Told Many Times

Jon Sobrino told us that the church in El Salvador was doing well in its priestly function, but there were no prophets at this time. Yet, there are actions by church people that seem as good and courageous and important as the actions of the Biblical prophets. The Reverend Norman Bent, a Moravian pastor who is from the Atlantic coast of Nicaragua, and who has a large church in Managua at this time is an example of one who speaks as a prophet.

The story of his work is one I have told often. We spent a day with Reverend Bent when he visited Princeton Theological Seminary as part of the continuing education program in the spring of 1987. As part of his talk he told us how his denomination had significant success in bringing about dialogue between the Nicaraguan Government and the Miskito Indian warriors who had fought the Sandinista Army after the revolution. Dialogue has led to peace, and to reconciliation. The indigenous people and the descendants of African slaves have an autonomy that is unique in all of Latin America. The parties themselves deserve the credit for the results, but the church deserves credit for its work to bring about the dialogue.

It was this dialogue that I referred to when I spoke with President Reagan. He and his aides know what has happened in Nicaragua when the church brought people together. It was this offer that I made, to help bring people together so that they can talk about peace. The Reagan Administration did not respond. I am not suggesting that I expected any other response, particularly in light of the efforts to fund the Contras legally and otherwise. Nevertheless, there appeared to be a role for the church and it was our role to tell the story.

The second time I told the story of the Moravian Church's efforts and successes in bringing about peace through dialogue was at a private party at which the guest of honor was a former United States Congressman. He had lost an attempt to be elected to the U.S. Senate. I told the same story, and made the same kind of plea that the church be heard in its attempt to help. The party was full of liberal Democrats, and their response was no more positive than that of the White House. No one even asked how we could accomplish anything.

I told this same story a third time. I was invited to Houston, Texas, to participate in an ecumenical dialogue with Congressman Bob Archer, a conservative Republican. There were 15 of us in the room with Archer and his wife and an aide. Once again I suggested that the church could do very positive things to bring about dialogue and peace. I told them of the work of Reverend Bent and the others. I challenged them to do something. Once again, the government leader did not respond. Once again, as well, the people of the church also did not respond.

The change in administration in the United States has not changed the problems of the people of Nicaragua, or elsewhere in Central America. Promises are still made and not kept. The Bush Administration has, in my opinion, placed distance between itself and the region. Part of this, I believe, is to permit activities to go on without public attention. Part, also, is that Mr. Bush does not have the emphasis on Central America that Mr. Reagan had during his terms as president.

Still, the poverty continues and so does the work of the church. To a large extent, the healing that has taken place on the Atlantic Coast of Nicaragua since the 1989 elections has been due to the continued work of the church. To the extent that division has occurred, it can be traced directly to those to whom promises were made and not kept, whether Contra or Sandinista. Promises of money and land have not been kept, and the country is drowning in poverty. Once again, the Moravian Church stands between those who have been misled and manipulated by those seeking power over the countryside.

What Will I Do?

It has been the experience of the participants in the struggle for peace with justice in Central America that dialogue with the government does not produce anything that can be called progress. It is our experience that we can not be political. We cannot be political because we must be much more than political. We must honor what Desmond Tutu says, that not taking sides is really taking sides with the established order. We are not political, because being political is not enough. The poor, and those who are being killed and starved and exploited, are not helped in any significant way by the political process.

In Managua, we gathered with many of the leading church representatives in Nicaragua. George Chauncey asked a theological question of the Nicaraguans who were present. He said, "What would God say to us in the United States if our Congress passes additional aid to the Contras?" This was only a few weeks before that most crucial vote.

One Nicaraguan said that his people look at the vote

as extremely serious for the fate of their country, but, like Daniel, they believe that God will not let the vote pass. None the less, if the vote passes and causes more death for their people, if they are, in a manner of speaking biblically, thrown into the furnace and consumed, they will still have faith in God.

Another theologian said that God would ask the same question that God asked of Cain, "Where is Abel, your brother?" He quoted further that God would say, "What have you done? The voice of your brother's blood is crying to me from the ground."

As we sat there, facing the word of God being used in such a real life situation so powerful that we could not even speak, Norman Bent, the Moravian pastor, said that he had a question for us. "If the vote passes," he asked, "what will you do?"

I said the only thing that I could. There was no other response possible from me. I said that if the vote passed, I would come down and stand with him. I could do no less. I was in solidarity with the people of Nicaragua, and I would have returned to Nicaragua if the vote had passed.

Those On The Other Side

Our dialogue with the government did not only concern Nicaragua. Most delegations have the opportunity to meet with leaders of these nations when they visit, depending upon the connections that the delegation leader has. A task force from the leadership of any denomination will often have the opportunity to visit with the president or other top officials of the nation. I have met President Duarte of El Salvador. I have also met President Violetta Chamorro before she was elected to that office in Nicaragua and I met President Alfredo Cristiani of El Salvador under a similar occasion prior to his election.

Both new presidents are under great pressure now, of

course. President Chamorro leads Nicaraguan attempts to assimilate the Contra and the Sandinista soldiers back into the ruined economy, after a cease fire and major political changes. President Cristiani is presiding over a country on the edge of a cease fire which may or may not include any significant political change. The people clearly want the civil war to end, although what the people want is seldom what they get. The government of El Salvador has not yet made that commitment and yet the people have not shown a willingness to support either side.

We have also met with leaders of the opposition. In Nicaragua, groups regularly met with the political leaders of the opposition to the Sandinista Administration. Now, of course, the Sandinistas are the opposition, but they are still accessible. More important, it was sometimes possible, particularly with Witness For Peace delegations, to meet with the Contra in the mountains under difficult and dangerous circumstances. I never had that opportunity. Now that they have come back and are taking a place in Nicaraguan society, opportunity for interviews exist. Those Contras who did the fighting have little voice in the course of events in Nicaragua, however.

In El Salvador, it is easier to meet with the opposition to the present government of that nation. In contrast to events in Nicaragua, the guerillas in El Salvador do control large parts of the countryside and can be seen openly in those areas. As the negotiations continue during the second half of 1991, delegations who have traveled in the country report seeing Salvadoran Government Army troops along a road and then in less than 5 miles seeing troops of the FMLN walking along that same road. It is possible to talk to soldiers on both sides of the civil war.

In a sense, when you talk with guerilla soldiers who are fighting an armed revolution or civil war, you are in dialogue with its government. At least it is a government that wishes to be, and if that army does control part of the countryside, it is functioning as a government. One can learn as much from soldiers as one does from politicians.

Learning From Soldiers

In 1990, we were in a small village which had been occupied by the Salvadoran Army at times and was in an area where the F.M.L.N. soldiers freely visited at the time when we were there. We were relaxing in the common building which served as meeting hall and church, among other things. That evening, a band was playing and some of the community was dancing while others talked or just sat, listening to the music.

I was sitting along one wall, relaxing and playing with a young child as he flirted, then sought the safety of his mother's skirts. I looked out on the dance floor and saw a young man in green fatigues and a black tee shirt. He was dancing with a young woman from the community. Next to him was a girl also in green fatigues and a black tee shirt, who was dancing with a young man. They were obviously having fun and no one paid special attention to them.

One of my group who had been outside came over to me, saying, "The Muchachoes are here. If you want to talk to them, come on out."

Outside, a group of people were talking next to a cement wall which had been decorated with F.M.L.N. writing. Several men and one more woman were dressed in black tee shirts. Each had guns which they were very careful with, so as not to threaten the rest of the group. In time, the guns were stacked, at the ready.

The conversation was easy and we talked about families and events. We were introducing ourselves and looking for things to talk about. I asked, "What message do you have for me to take back to the United States?"

One young man smiled and said, "We will never stop fighting until there is justice in El Salvador." Others clapped or shouted agreement. Then he asked, "Do you have children?'

"Yes," I responded.

"Do you want another one?"

"Why do you ask," I said.

"I will be your son. I will come to the United States with you and go to school. I will be your son and go to U.C.L.A." He laughed. "I will even study."

"Then you will stop fighting?"

"For a while. I'll study and come back, better prepared." Someone else asked a question and the moment was gone.

The next day, as we walked fields and looked at projects, our translator asked if we wanted to have a formal meeting with the guerillas. The F.M.L.N. soldiers from last night were in a small structure, with two men standing guard outside. The way they carried their guns was much more intense now. The building was part lean-to and part shack. We said yes and went in.

We heard a presentation from a slightly older leader. What he said about the issues and the conflict, and what he said about their resolve and sense of justice, was well presented but not new. What was new was what came out in bits and pieces as we had time for questions. The leader had been at the University, I can only guess at which one, and had combined his education with his observations of life in El Salvador. He told us briefly how the pull of other organizers and recruiters increased, and how he decided that the reality of El Salvador did not promise life. His expectations of basic human dignity were not lived out in what he saw and heard.

He told us that he could not deny the humanity of his family and friends. They were poor but they were people who deserved to have food, shelter, water, clothing. They even deserved justice, he said. That, to me, was his compelling argument.

This interview was one of those times in life when it

was very difficult for me not to be clearly on one side of the conflict, rather than to be seeking peace between sides. This was a time when I realized that rational and reasoned acknowledgment of the issues may not be enough in the face of tragic reality. This was a time in my conversion process when I could affirm that not taking sides is impossible, for to do nothing, to observe but not participate, was to side with the status quo. And the status quo was not very easy for most of the people of El Salvador.

The F.M.L.N. officer was human for those moments, not just a gun carrying soldier who brought death to the other side. I had to wonder if this man was one of the hungry, naked, oppressed who Christ spoke of in the story of the sheep and the goats, in Matthew 25. It was not possible to ignore the man as a person. It was possible to see beyond the black tee shirt and green fatigues of his uniform.

I did not ask for a gun, and I have no intention of taking arms on behalf of anyone. My understanding of Christ's response to the hungry and naked and oppressed is not violence. Rather, the response is one of accompaniment, and of being willing to give one's own life for another. Perhaps this is why I was able later in the week to challenge the Salvadoran Army. I was able to be a participant, in solidarity and without a gun.

Crossing Borders Together

Solidarity is a word which is used by many people to describe certain relationships. In Latin America, and particularly in El Salvador, it is used to describe the relationship between the north, represented by delegations from the first world, and the south, represented by the poor in the third world. At events where both are present, one hears the cry in Spanish, "Viva solidarity with the Internationals!" We respond, "Que Viva!" We heard many shouts of "Viva!" during our day at the University of Central

America, during the time honoring the martyrs of El Salvador.

The day after the meeting with the activists and those in solidarity with them, we were supposed to be in accompaniment. We were supposed to be part of a repopulation, in which a small group of refugees were to return to their land of origin. I was apprehensive. I wrote in my notebook: "I don't know if it is a good idea [to go on this repopulation], but we do what we can. So, now, it is the last full day in El Salvador and we need to find peace in solidarity. This is the last place on earth where justice has a chance."

Before this trip, the Philadelphia homeless delegation met to organize and to get to know each other. At the very first meeting, one of the delegation members caught the vision. She said, "I can see it now. They're going to say, my God, they're crossing borders together!" This statement was an immediate identification between the poor and oppressed of the repopulation and repatriation movement of El Salvador with the homeless struggle in the United States. It was the first step to solidarity, and it was prophetic.

None of our delegation is truly at risk in our daily lives back home. When we look at the risks and dangers of working for peace, or feeding one's family, and simply staying alive that the Salvadorans face, we know we are not persecuted. If we are not one of those who are persecuted for righteousness' sake, how can the kingdom of heaven be ours? If we want to participate in the kingdom of God, we must be in physical solidarity with those who are persecuted, even killed. We must seek this physical solidarity, even at the risk of our lives. We must respond and do that which we preached the day before.

We said that we believed in this solidarity in San Salvador at a meeting at the University of Central America. Salvadorans and North Americans were in solidarity with the struggles of the poor in El Salvador. We said it, but so many things are said in safety. It was a fair question to ask if we meant what we said.

That day, about 15 trucks and vans formed a caravan of Salvadorans and North Americans traveling to San Vicente Province. This was the first repopulation in this Province, and our delegation went along, to accompany the poor. It has not been the last.

The Captured Truck

Before we arrived at the location of repopulation, we received word that a truck loaded with building supplies and food had been taken by the military. A small delegation of four North Americans and a Salvadoran translator was sent to the military post to see what we could do. Another jeep followed, with some of the people from the repopulation.

We found the truck under guard at the San Vicente headquarters of this Brigade of the Salvadoran Army. We were taken to meet Salvadoran Major Monico, who said he was in charge of the matter. We entered into dialogue, negotiating for the release of the truck and supplies.

Major Monico explained that we were to respect the law in El Salvador, just as he would respect it in the United States. He told us that the law required us to have either written title to the land, or written permission from the land owner, or written permission from the Salvadoran Government.

We replied that we always kept the law and that we owned the building supplies. It was really the Salvadorans who were going to use the supplies. They should determine where they would be building their homes. We wanted to respect the law, but what kind of law would keep people from returning to where they were born? This was truly dialogue with the government.

The negotiations ended as we were told to call the High Command, using a public phone down the street. We left, and called people in San Salvador who would contact groups back in the United States, who had agreed to help us with telephone calls if we encountered any difficulty. We also reported that the larger delegation of 15 vehicles was being detained by armed military soldiers.

Under orders from the Army, the caravan of trucks and vans came into town and joined us, a block from the Military Offices. The whole North American contingent of over 50 persons gathered together, while our negotiating team began to talk again with Major Monico.

During the first negotiation session, we had come through the large double doors and walked back to an office, in relative privacy. During the second session, we stayed in sight of the double doors. Several of the group decided that we might be in danger and blocked the doorway, so that the soldiers with their M-16 rifles were unable to close the doors. The North Americans formed a large circle and began to sing. Major Monico was not happy.

At that time, a North American in jeans and a dress shirt arrived, and demanded to know who was in charge. Since we were an ecumenical group, no one was in charge. The man identified himself as Major Joseph Andrade, United States Army military advisor.

Major Andrade entered the negotiations, first with the negotiating team and then outside with the larger delegation. He explained the law, as Major Monico had previously done. Someone said that the title to the land had been destroyed by bombs, in fact by bombs which had been dropped with U.S. military advice. Major Andrade became angry and went back inside with the Salvadoran military and the elected negotiating team.

The second round of negotiations ended with a small group being delegated to call the U.S. Embassy and the High Command of the Salvadoran Military, again at a public phone around the corner. They left, and there was a period of song and prayer outside while discussions went on inside. The doors were still held open by unarmed women and men in the face of soldiers carrying M-16s.

Protest Songs And Dance

It was clear that negotiations were taking place on two levels. Logic was presented by both sides, and politely discarded. At the same time, pressure was being applied. The songs and prayers outside were drawing a crowd. A military employee came with a video camera, and photographed the delegation. Telephone calls began coming from the United States, and other calls went from Embassy to High Command to this military post in San Vicente. Salvadoran Colonel Carpio was now giving orders, quietly, although Major Monico remained the spokesman for the military. Major Andrade was giving advice.

It was not clear what would happen, and several of us on the negotiating team were called back into the military post. We went back to the small office and waited. After a while, the Embassy called and spoke with one of our group. Major Monico was not in the office, but we were joined by U.S. Major Andrade and Salvadoran Colonel Carpio.

Another call came in, and we were told that Colonel Ponce was on the telephone. Colonel Ponce, the Salvadoran Defense Minister, was and is the highest ranking military person in El Salvador. He spoke with Colonel Carpio for a while, in a quiet conversation.

After that, it was all over. We were given permission to take the truck full of building supplies and go anywhere we wanted to go. Someone was asked to sign for the supplies and a Salvadoran woman, tears in her eyes, came forward to sign for them. The military can check on what has been done with the supplies at any time now. We were free to go.

The caravan that left the town of San Vicente drove off like a victory parade. There was joy in all the trucks and vans. There was also some admiration from the people on the streets. We drove to the planned location for the repopulation and the truck was unloaded.

How To Respond To A Threat

There was a time during the negotiations when Major Monico said that we should leave this repopulation to them because, he said, they have the expertise in arms and guns. We asked if he was threatening us with talks of guns. He said that he was not threatening us. We replied that this was not a matter for guns but for the rights of the people. He had no reply.

It is generally conceded that others in the Salvadoran military were involved in some way in the death of the 6 Jesuits and 2 women the year before. Though knees may shake and tears may fall, those killings had not stopped the Salvadorans and North Americans from being in solidarity. When guns are your only way to persuade, what do you do when the other side remains unarmed? Perhaps this repopulation was a major victory for solidarity and for the efforts of non-violent refusal to give in when justice is at stake. This was what was being said: The Army has killed others, perhaps not these soldiers personally, and we are still here.

In a sense, the combined work of the delegations and the Salvadoran people produced the victory for repopulation efforts. It was also a defeat for the military. The military had to either back down from their position and allow repopulation or they had to use their guns. This time they didn't know what to do. We did cross borders together.

One of the Salvadorans who had been part of all the events of the last two days shook my hand. He said, "Yesterday you said some very nice things. Today you put it in practice. That is what is important."

There really was solidarity between Salvadoran and North American, between homeless who are displaced by a war and homeless who are displaced by a policy implementing that war. It was physical solidarity.

It was not easy. One of the four negotiators was a Jesuit from California. He said that after it was all over his knees shook for five minutes. He was in solidarity with those in the delegation, but also with those six Jesuits who were honored just three days before for their martyrdom. Yet he took part in the dialogue with the government.

7

BEYOND OBSERVER

It has been made clear that one encounters both suffering and joy in the presence of the radical, systemic evil in Central America. Our experience of this has been further shaped for us by dialogue with the larger church and the government bringing about a process of transformation. These experiences can provide a basis for a theology in which God's word is encountered, at a time when there is a real sense of the demonic. Through this word God gives a call for a prophetic response.

This book has been written to North Americans, particularly from the United States, so that they can see and hear the people with whom God is found. It is an attempt to be a voice of many voices, crying out to be heard. It is not written for those in the United States who listen and then say, "Yes, but what about my interests?" I would like to reach them but they will have to make the trip themselves to have ears to hear.

The stories and events which are related in this book

come from people who place the interests of others ahead of their own interest. There are many people who have listened to us speak and with whom we have been in dialogue over the past six years. Some have even trusted us enough to travel with us to Central America. Often they ask, "How can this be?" and often they say, "I didn't know."

The title, *Voice Of Many Crying*, is a reference to the Biblical person, John the Baptist, and the preparations he made for the ministry of Jesus. At a Christian Base Community in Managua, the community was talking about the day when Jesus was baptized by John and God said, *"Thou art my beloved Son; with thee I am well pleased."* (Luke 3:22)

We were expected to say something, and all I could think to say was that every time I came to Central America, I felt like I was one of the throng of people on the banks of the River Jordan, watching but not being part of the new ministry. My only hope, I said, was that I would be one of those who would follow Jesus.

No one in the church pointed out that all of Jesus' followers deserted him, including the apostles. They did, however, suggest that if I would follow Jesus, I would be expected to pick up my cross! To the extent that I have picked up my cross, I am a voice of many crying. And those who cry out echo the words of Archbishop Oscar Romero, just days before he was martyred. "In the name of God, stop the killing."

Once Again A Voice

After all the dialogue with the Salvadoran and United States Governments in San Vicente on that last day in El Salvador for the Philadelphia homeless delegation, we finally reached the small field where the food and water and building supplies were to be used to rebuild a community. It is to be called Communidad Padre Macias, in memory of a martyred priest.

A priest was there and offered a prayer. He spoke again about the visitors to the baby Jesus, recorded in Matthew 2:1-2:

> *Now when Jesus was born in Bethlehem of Judea in the days of Herod the king, behold wise men from the East came to Jerusalem, saying, "Where is he who has been born king of the Jews? For we have seen his star in the East, and have come to worship him."*

I thought a lot about the choice of the Biblical image. Once again there is reference to the visit of the wise men, just as there had been at the mass in El Barrio, on my first visit. This time I had enough sense to keep my mouth shut about denying our role. I had come a long way in my conversion from observer to participant. I had crossed borders with the poor. I had stood inside the military post and was not afraid.

When I got up that morning, I felt like staying home. What could I do at a repopulation? But I went because it was important to do what we said we would do. Some call that walking our talk.

It Would Be Nice

It would be nice to say that somehow we have figured out how to solve the problems of Central America and that all that is needed is to listen to us to find the "keys" to that "kingdom." But this is not possible. We were only visitors in a region that has a different view of the kingdom, based upon a mixture of centuries of Roman Catholic religious leadership and very recent evangelical prosperity preaching.

It would be nice to say that somehow we have been able to figure out how to change or adjust United States policy to help bring about peace to the region of Central America. That is, of course, not the case since we were not even able to give such programmatic answers to President Reagan when we had the dialogue in the White House. At that meeting, the best we could do was offer to help work for peace, to bring people together under Christ.

It would even be nice to say that somehow we have brought people together in a common understanding of what God would have us do in our church. That is also, unfortunately, not the case. Yet it is here that we do make our contribution to the work of the church. It is in discerning what God would have us do and how that is expressed where we really make a contribution. Speaking to the church, calling for all to pray and fast, to study and visit, to advocate and to listen, we speak of a theology. The theology itself does not bring the church together, but with it we ask the church to come together in dialogue to seek God first and not ourselves.

What Would God Say?

At the time of my first visit, I had no idea that I would be changed, transformed really, from an observer to a participant in the life of the people of Central America. I had yet to experience what was ahead of me and what I have described in capsule form as the salient points of that experience. That experience is behind me now, as I join others who speak from this common experience.

In one word, both the experience and the theology can be described by the Greek word *metanoia*. *Metanoia* is often translated in Mark 1:4 as *repent* and is translated in the Spanish Bible I bought on that trip as *cambien su vida.*.

Much has been written about *metanoia*, interpreting a word that includes the concept of a change of heart and mind away from self and sin, and toward God and holiness. The Spanish, *cambien su vida* can be literally translated into English as *change your life*. I can't say if there is greater meaning in the Spanish than my literal translation. Each language and each culture adds much richness to a word or phrase. In English, it may also be translated as change your mind.

The Greek word has been chosen because it includes the concept of repentance, and is larger than the more common English word of repent. I also want to avoid the word "conversion" which has a more personal connotation in present theological thinking and writing. It is a word that Jesus used and was recorded in Mark's Gospel as the kingdom of God was announced. We still seek that kingdom. The experience of suffering and joy in the presence of radical systemic evil, and the shaping of the experiences in dialogue with the larger church and the government, is ultimately a community experience in which others are put ahead of our own needs, as we love one another as Jesus has loved us. The reflection and the theological understanding is *metanoia*.

A change of heart and mind away from self and sin and toward God and people and holiness takes place when one's life is truly changed in this manner. *Metanoia* happens through the hearing of God's word, in the face of a society that strives to silence that word, by responding to the word, to say yes to God and to say no to false gods.

God Said......

The first element of *metanoia*, God's word, acts as a call to listen, as though a prophet stands before us, saying as Isaiah did, *God said*. We are invited to *Hear the Word of the Lord*. The voice of the prophet is not the North American who comes down to a poor country, proclaiming the gospel. The gospel is personalized in Central America as the people identify with the Biblical stories. When Jesus visited Zaccheus, he didn't think about personal danger but only how he could help. We see Central Americans urge each other to do the same, even as they fast for peace and justice.

There is a strong power being exerted in Central America against those who tried to speak God's word. This strong power is used against those who speak and those who would listen to what God says. While there are many names for this power, it is most clearly expressed by a real sense of the demonic in forces that would control the region. This is another element of *metanoia* in which there is a recognition that humanity is not only prone to sin individually. Humanity is prone to sin in a systemic manner which directly and adversely affects those who are not directly responsible. Those affected may even be innocent. They may be guilty of individual sin, as all people are, but there is a presence of systemic evil that seems to seek indiscriminate destruction and is opposed to creation. It is a demonic presence. While it is everywhere, it is most seen among the affluent and powerful.

There is no way for the conditions of the people to exist to the extent that they do without the knowledge and permission of the structure of society. The government and the church, to the extent it does not oppose the repression, have combined with those in power to oppose much that is good for the sake of keeping in power those who control the organizations. To see that power in use is to experience a sense of the demonic, and the only response is to call for repentance. There is a clear understanding that a prophetic response is needed to bring about repentance.

To Transform The World

The message that we bring back from our transformation from observer to participant is, after all, analogous to the message brought back by the kings who visited the baby Jesus in Bethlehem. We recognize that there is an incarnational presence somewhere, and we find it in the faces of those who cry out. We become their voice, the voice of many crying.

In effect, we no longer seek to explain the Biblical message to the world. No longer are we satisfied to preach the Gospel. Now, we are forced by our own convictions and by the convictions of those we meet to actually try to live the Gospel.

Both Latin American liberation theology and Latin American fundamentalism seek to transform the world to the Bible, rather than to explain the Bible to the world as many liberals and North American evangelicals do. I wish this observation was my own but it is not. In his book, *Religion in the Secular City*, published by Simon and Schuster, New York, 1984, Professor Harvey Cox states that, "One might say that liberal and evangelical theologians have tried to make the Christian message credible to the modern world. Fundamentalists and liberation theologians are not interested in interpreting. They do not want to speak to and be heard by the world so much as they want to change it."

A major point in Cox's book is that post-modern theology will come from the bottom and the edges of society. That may be true, as it was in earliest Christianity, and in the days of the prophets of Israel. As in the days of the prophets of the Bible, society was called upon to hear the word of God, to recognize the presence of the demonic in their midst, and to respond with prophetic acts. Certainly it comes from the prophetic voice of those who are martyred, whether famous as the Jesuits have become or unknown outside the immediate family, as a child is who dies of measles in Nicaragua because there no longer is vaccine.

The Reality Of Sin

Professor Jon Sobrino, S.J., is a voice I have heard speak for the voiceless, in person and in his writings. In the April 3, 1991 issue of <u>The Christian Century</u>, he writes about his own transition from observer to participant, using his own words of "Awakening from the sleep of inhumanity". Sobrino quotes his friend and martyr Father Ignacio Ellacuría, Rector of the University of Central America in El Salvador and one of those who were murdered. Father Ellacuría referred to "entire crucified peoples" as he spoke of the millions of poverty stricken people in this world. Two thirds of the world is poor, and starving, and without adequate shelter and clothing and medicine.

Sobrino says that, "One may or may not believe in God, but because of the reality of death no one will be able to deny the reality of sin." This reality of sin, and the causes of the reality of death are set over against the reality of God as a choice. One can only speak the truth if one not only identifies the God in which one believes, but one must also identify the idols in which one does not believe. Otherwise, faith remains too abstract.

It is difficult to illustrate faith in God and no faith in idols, and yet we must try to do that, to draw that distinction. When we confronted the Salvadoran military, and had dialogue with the United States Army major and, indirectly and by telephone the United States Embassy in El Salvador, we expressed our faith in God by accompanying the refugees who sought to rebuild their homes. We did this by placing ourselves on the other side of a debate in which guns and death had been used. Major Monico told us to leave the business of guns to the military. We responded by saying that the death of six Jesuits and two pious women, and 75,000 others in El Salvador would not deter us from our demands.

Some of us were frightened. Remember the Jesuit who told of his knees shaking. Some of us didn't want to be there. I was one who almost didn't accompany the people. And yet all of us stood fast and prayed. We said, by our actions and by our words, that we have come here and we have no guns. We want justice and you can do what you must. We refused to bow to the idols of death and violence. We refused to turn our faces away from those with whom we have had true incarnational experiences. There was nothing abstract about our faith that day.

Professor Sobrino says this about faith. "What Christian faith says is that God will grant definitive justice to the victims of poverty and, by extension, to those who have sided with them. This is an active hope which unloosens creativity at all levels of human existence -- intellectual, organizational, ecclesial -- and which is marked by notable generosity and boundless, even heroic altruism."

A Moment In History

The experience in San Vicente was a moment in history, and most of us have returned to safer lands. The poor are still seeking to build homes in the midst of a war, but now, at least some of them know that their story is being told. Our experience was their experience, and out of the common experience was both joy and suffering in the midst of radical systemic evil.

Professor Sobrino says one more thing that I want to quote. In the article in The Christian Century, he talks about new questions which he asked, and radically different answers. "The basic question came to be: Are we really human and, if we are believers, is our faith human? The reply was not the anguish which follows an awakening from dogmatic sleep, but the joy which comes when we are willing not only to change our minds from enslavement to liberation, but also to change our vision in order to see what had been there, unnoticed, all along, and to change hearts of stone into hearts of flesh--in other words, to let ourselves be moved to compassion and mercy."

Are we really human? Are we able to look at poverty and suffering and disease and hunger and death and orphans and widows and prisoners, and do nothing? The world which we describe, of the plight of two thirds of humanity, is a desperate world. It is the world of first century Palestine, and the world of a conquered nation of Israel, into which God entered, taking on the form of a servant, born in human form, obedient unto death, even death on the cross. [Phil.2:7-8]

Turn Your Eyes Upon Jesus

There is a chorus we sing which says,

Turn your eyes upon Jesus.
Look full in his wonderful face, and the things of
earth will grow strangely dim,
in the light of his glory and grace.

These words are not directed inwardly toward a contemplative life, in which spiritual discipline will show us the face of Jesus. How do we see Jesus?

To start, we must go to where Jesus is. Remember once again the words of Professor Jon de Cortina, S.J., who told us that "If God is not with the poor of El Salvador, then God is nowhere." So to see Jesus, we must go to the people with whom God is present. But that is not enough.

We must turn our eyes on Jesus, and look into the face of Jesus and into the eyes of Jesus. We have to see the tears in the eyes of Jesus in order to look full in his wonderful face. If we can look past our first world security and if we can recognize the humanity of the poor, in El Salvador or anywhere in the world, we can see Jesus.

When our homeless delegation visited the Romero Chapel on the campus of the University of Central America in San Salvador, I sat with Hilda, an African-American woman from Chester, Pennsylvania. She looked up at the cross, and over at the tombs of the Jesuits, and then at the back wall where obscene paintings hung, of torture and mutilation and death. She pointed to the paintings and said, "Now I understand. That happened to my people."

> God says, *"Where is he who has been born*
> *king of the Jews? For we have seen his star in the*
> *East, and have come to worship him."*

Not only are we to worship Jesus, we are to tell his story. We are to tell the Gospel. We are to be a voice, a voice of many crying. And we need to see their tears.

AFTERWORD

When a person's life symbolizes an ideal, it is fitting to give tribute to that life. Philip Mitchell's life symbolizes the total conversion which people of faith experience when they hear the voice of the poor cry out to them. The Reverend Gary Campbell has adapted the following from an article originally written in Spanish for the Nov.-Dec. issue of the magazine *AMANACER*. It is a memorial to Phil Mitchell, a Christian who lived the life of one who truly was transformed from Observer to Participant. Gary is a friend and colleague of Philip Mitchell, and a mission co-worker of the Presbyterian Church (USA) serving at the Antonio Valdivieso Ecumenico Center in Managua, Nicaragua. Gary has worked in Latin America for nearly 30 years.

IN MEMORIUM
Philip Mitchell
(February 17, 1943 - November 22, 1991)

I met Philip Mitchell and his wife Nan McCurdy-Mitchell for the first time in August 1986 when my wife Chess and I accompanied an ecumenical delegation to San Juan de Limay, in the Department of Esteli, Nicaragua. Chess and I had arrived in Managua just a few days before to live and work in our new assignment to Nicaragua. Nan and Phil had arrived about a year earlier to initiate an ecumenical sistering relationship between the community of San Juan de Limay and the St. John's United Methodist Church in Baltimore, Maryland. In that first experience with Phil, I felt admiration for this young couple who had given up their comfortable and secure life in the U.S.A. to cast their lot with poor Nicaraguan campesinos in a war zone. In that first encounter and always afterwards we discovered in Phil and Nan a spirit of joy and love of life. In seeing how Phil related to members of the U.S. delegation as well as to Nicaraguan friends, I was impressed with his special gifts of gentleness, sensitivity and compassion.

After three years in Limay assisting in community development and their pastoral accompaniment of friends grieved by the disappearances and murders, in 1988 Phil and Nan moved to Managua and were assigned as United Methodist missionaries to the Antonio Valdivieso Center (CAV) to work in the area of solidarity. In visits to Managua before their move from Limay they often stayed with us. Shortly after the murder in northern Nicaragua of U.S. civil engineer Benjamin Linder in April 1987, Phil suggested a U.S. citizens solidarity center to be named in honor of Ben. That idea materialized with the opening of Casa Benjamin Linder in January 1989.

Philip Mitchell died on Friday morning, November 22, 1991, at the Alejandro Davila Hospital in Managua, Nicaragua. The autopsy report indicated that massive pulmonary emboli had been the cause of death. Exactly one month earlier he had vascular surgery on his left leg at the same hospital. Medical checks a few days before showed that Phil was recuperating well from the surgery. That morning he was getting ready to return to his work at CAV after one month's absence.

This news came on top of the news that Padre Cesar Jerez S.J. (age 55), friend of CAV and President of the Central

American University (UCA) in Managua had died earlier that same morning in Columbia, South America, also from natural causes.

The emotions of disbelief, grief and sadness make it difficult to express adequately the feelings and thoughts of all of us who have been hurt by these deaths. Scripture comes to mind, particularly for our memory of Phil Mitchell. We look to the Gospel according to St. Luke, where we read:

> *Jesus said to him [the rich young man]: "There is still one thing lacking. Sell all that you own and distribute the money to the poor." But when he heard this, he became sad.(Luke 18:22-23)*
> *AND*
> *Then Jesus said to him [Zaccheus]: "Today salvation has come to this house." (Luke 19:9)*

Thanks to the memories of many moments, experiences, words of faith and hope, there is inspiration and motivation to write this modest and brief testimony to the memory of Phil Mitchell's life, faith and faithfulness. His story is not that of the rich young man unable to accept Jesus' requirements but rather the history of a successful young artist and businessman who, like Zaccheus, said 'yes' to Jesus' demands. And the hospitable McCurdy-Mitchell home filled with Phil's joy and that of an extraordinary wife and two precious children, Phil no doubt heard those words of divine grace: *Today salvation has come to this house.* Phil's story is the story of a disciple of Jesus Christ who came to be brother and compañero of all those in this land and elsewhere struggling for that revolutionary Gospel which promises a new life, a just life, a life in abundance for the poor of the earth.

The ecumenical memorial service for Phil was celebrated Saturday, November 23 in La Merced Catholic Church in the Barrio Larreynaga. I shared leadership of the service with United Methodist pastor and missionary Lyda Pierce and Catholic priests Antonio Castro and Uriel Molina. In addition to the ecumenical celebration of Holy Communion, the service included songs from the famous Campesino Mass of Nicaragua led by the Galo family musical group, readings and reflections about two passages from the Gospel of Luke, quoted above, and testimonies by friends and compañeros. During a period of community reflection, former President Daniel Ortega, who sat beside the family, observed how Nicaragua had lost two great international friends in Cesar Jerez and Phil Mitchell, each of them involved in distinct vocations and situations but both committed to the same preferential option for the poor.

One day later the graveside service was celebrated in the Occidental Cemetery of Managua. The graveside service consisted of Scripture, prayers, religious and popular songs from El Salvador and Nicaragua and also English hymns/songs like *Amazing Grace, Danny Boy,* and the South African song of struggle, *We Shall Not Give Up The Fight.* Just before Nan's final "goodbye Phil," she sang *Because Of You,* a favorite popular love song which she said was one of many the two of them would often sing to each other, demonstrating as she sang beside his grave remarkable strength, courage and love. Both services were experiences of profound grief but at the same time inspiring celebrations of faith and hope.

In the years 1963 to 1964 Phil Mitchell worked in Chile as a volunteer with the Peace Corps. He signed up after hearing President John F. Kennedy famous "Ask not what your country can do for you, ask what you can do for your country" speech at his college, San Diego State, in 1962. (Like Phil and Padre Cesar Jerez, JFK also died on November 22.) In the immediate six years before coming with Nan to Nicaragua, Phil had owned successful advertising and publishing design businesses. On recalling that history during the funeral service, the Rev. Paul Jeffrey, CEPAD journalist and United Methodist missionary commented, "Phil always reminded people who knew him of the possibility that U.S. citizens trapped in consumerist, middle-class lifestyles can experience a radical conversion to the Gospel of Jesus Christ....Along with the people of Limay and the rest of Nicaragua, we will miss Phil, but we will remember fondly his intolerance with injustice and lies, his impatience for bringing the reign of God, and his love for this little country and its revolution. He represented the best of the people of the United States."

All of his friends at CAV will continue to suffer the incalculable loss of our friend and compañero Filepe Mitchell. And just as he accompanied many Nicaraguan friends in the loss of parents, spouses and children, so we will continue to accompany Nan, Daniel and Nora and all the family in their times of grief and also in their times of celebrating that life which enriched all of us and will continue to enrich us.

FILEPE MITCHELL
PRESENTE! PRESENTE! PRESENTE!

Gary Campbell
Managua, Nicaragua